This playbook belongs to:

_____

If found, please return to this address:

_____

_____

Hi, Kids!

WagiLabs is endorsed by:

NATIONAL
AfterSchool
ASSOCIATION

"WagiLabs provides a free open-source curriculum, train-the-teacher sessions, and a collaborative community for our kids in Nigeria to develop and implement their socially innovative ideas."

— Temitope Kalejaiye,
Amnesty International Broadcast Journalist

"WagiLabs are a perfect complement to YWCA Metropolitan Chicago's programs because they encourage our girls to create innovative solutions to pervasive social problems while developing empathy in the process."

— Shelley Bromberek-Lambert,
Chief Reimagination Officer YWCA

"Our teachers love WagiLabs and are learning as much as the kids. It is transforming how we teach."

— Pamela Stepko, Assistant Principal
Cumberland County Elementary School

 A Special Thank You:

Diane Foucar-Szocki and Nick Swayne at James Madison University, Molly Hughes and Melissa Levy at University of Virginia, James Orrigo, Lexi Hutchins, Blaire Denson at V-Post, Carl Brown at DTRA; Jennifer Tyrell, Jennifer Casey, Kayla Canario and Chris Nelson at ORISE; Amy Griffin, Pamela Stepko, Ginny Gills and Kim Williamson at CCPS; Jennifer McKendree and Bethany Bogacki at Operation Smile, Mary Power, Larry Thompson, Kathy Kinter, Cat Beach, David Durovy

Contents

The KidpreneurSHIP

Discover more about yourself, the world, and the power of ideas to improve lives!

Welcome!

All kids love empty boxes — especially big ones from large appliances. Kids can turn a box into anything they imagine by saying these magic words:

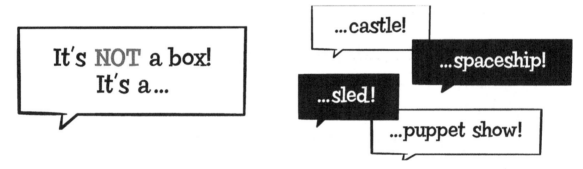

It's NOT a box!
It's a...

...castle!

...spaceship!

...sled!

...puppet show!

Wagi, our mascot, believes in this same world of endless possibilities. He invites kids to unleash their wildly creative ideas in WagiLabs!

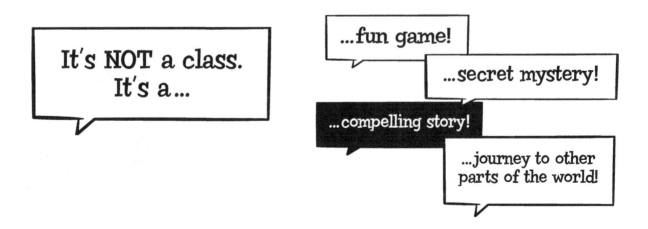

It's NOT a class.
It's a...

...fun game!

...secret mystery!

...compelling story!

...journey to other parts of the world!

What is WagiLabs?

WagiLabs are incubators for kids' ideas. They are all about play — and ideas. Most importantly, **doing good** to help people, animals, and the environment.

Our labs are part laboratory, part workshop, and all-around playgrounds for discovery. When kids play and create together, their imaginations come together, and new ideas happen!

WagiLabs are designed especially for kids in **elementary schools** and **afterschool programs**.

We link every WagiLabs in the U.S. with an international lab. By pairing these "WagiWorlds," we promote empathy and global perspective in our kids.

Environment is no obstacle for us — we can build a WagiLabs at school, on a bus or in a tree. Sharing ideas, learning from each other, and making people's lives better — that's the spirit of WagiLabs.

Watch the founder of WagiLabs, Chic Thompson's, TED Talk at:

https://bit.ly/2w7Y8vH

What is a Kidpreneur?

A kid who uses curiosity, compassion, and courage to come up with ideas to solve challenges in their community and the world.

Curiosity + Compassion + Courage
= Change the World

Curiosity is the mindset of a Kidpreneur. The urge to invent is contagious, especially between the ages of 8-11.

Compassion is the heart of a Kidpreneur. The kids learn empathy by walking in others' shoes and identifying community needs.

Courage is the strength of a Kidpreneur. The kids ask challenging questions, brainstorm multiple solutions, and risk making mistakes.

In today's world, competitive markets demand more and better ideas, and the skills to collaborate on these ideas.

Jobs that are disappearing today will be reinvented by Kidpreneurs tomorrow. We want our WagiKids to lead the way!

Who is Wagi?

Wagi, our mascot, comes from a long line of creative canines with a mission to do good things. The letters in "Wagi" stand for the words in the phrase, **"What a Great Idea!"**

What a GREAT Idea!

Wagi is on a journey to make the world better — and he needs our help!

Wagi loves great ideas, especially ideas from kids. That's why he created WagiLabs. He leads each mission and reminds us to dream big, do good, be kind, share ideas, and keep going until we reach our goals.

Wagi's inspirational messages are called the **"WagiWays."**

Map of Our WagiVoyage

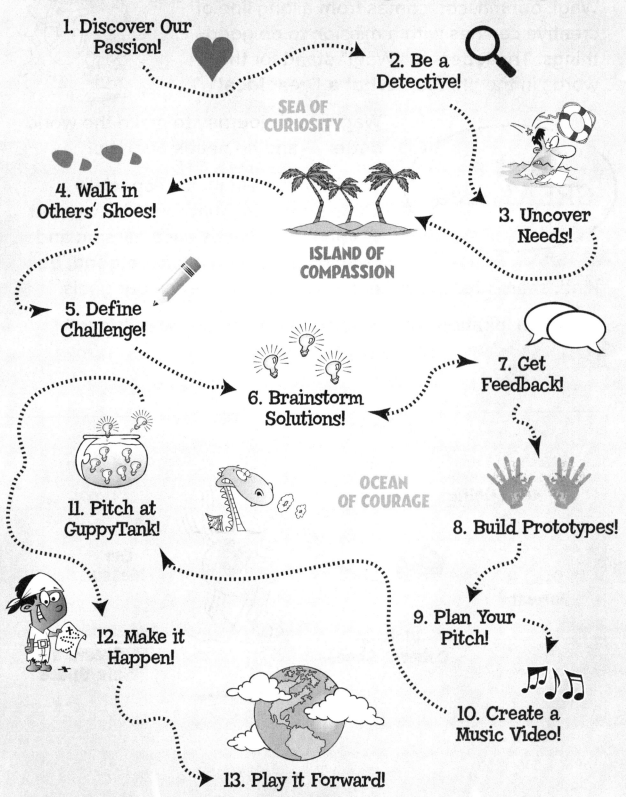

1. Discover Our Passion!

2. Be a Detective!

SEA OF CURIOSITY

3. Uncover Needs!

4. Walk in Others' Shoes!

ISLAND OF COMPASSION

5. Define Challenge!

6. Brainstorm Solutions!

7. Get Feedback!

OCEAN OF COURAGE

8. Build Prototypes!

11. Pitch at GuppyTank!

9. Plan Your Pitch!

12. Make it Happen!

10. Create a Music Video!

13. Play it Forward!

The adventure begins.
You are meeting the

Crew of Connection!

Your mission will be to:

☐ Learn the WagiWays

The WagiWays give teachers and kids direction in how to work together. They are the values that everyone at WagiLabs tries to live by every day.

☐ Create a Safe Space

We make sure to create a safe space for discovery because every kid has a great idea inside of them, just waiting to be revealed.

☐ Understand Roles and Goals

When we know what the goal is, we can look at our strengths and see how we can help.

☐ Stop and Pop!

Learn to recognize your feelings and calm your thoughts through practicing Mindfulness.

☐ WagiSTEM

We will be using **science**, **technology**, **engineering**, and **mathematics** exercises with our crew to help chart the course.

Learn the WagiWays!

1. **Create a Safe Space:** We start by being kind to ourselves and each other.

2. **Dream Big:** We brainstorm a lot of amazing ideas — there are no limits to our creativity!

3. **Yes, AND:** We always say: "Yes, **AND**..." when someone shares an idea. That means "I hear your idea ... **AND** I'm ready to learn more and add my ideas to make it grow!

4. **Walk-in Others' Shoes:** We imagine what other people's lives are like by "**trying on their shoes**" so we can see the world through their eyes. Having compassion is how we understand the changes that are needed in the world.

5. **Do Good:** We remember to focus on ideas that will make life better for our community and the world.

6. **Get Messy:** We build prototypes of our best ideas. We conduct experiments and learn through trial and error.

7. **Keep Going:** We never give up. We keep trying to build and sell our ideas, even when we face obstacles. We bounce back and try different solutions when our first try doesn't work.

8. **Play It Forward:** We leave footprints that become a pathway to invention for kids around the world.

What are the Rules at WagiLabs?

At each WagiLabs, the kids create the rules.

List five things you could do to make sure you don't have fun or learn anything at WagiLabs. We've filled in the first one for you!

1. Don't tell anyone my ideas.

2. _____

3. _____

4. _____

5. _____

Now, look at the five ideas on your list. What are the "opposite" things you could do? Write them here.

1. Share my ideas with everyone.

2. _____

3. _____

4. _____

5. _____

Aha! Can you see how flipping your thinking changes everything? The five ideas on your "opposites" list will be your rules to follow.

Create a "Safe Space"

You can do it!

Listen to the Parrot!

Do you see the colorful parrot sitting on Capt. Wagi's nose. His name is "Chati."

What are the phrases that Chati hears and repeats on the KidpreneurShip? If the phrases are:

1. Dream big!

2. Yes, **AND**...

3. You can do it!

4. That was fun!

You have a safe space for kids to create ideas and be themselves while learning.

If the phrases are:

1. That will never work!

2. That was stupid!

3. You're weird!

4. Non-verbal "rolled eyes"

Then you have a space with fear and most kids will not feel comfortable to participate in group exercises.

To help turn a "never work" to a **"let's make it work,"** Wagi wants you to respond to:

"That will never work!" with
"What will it take to make it work?"

"That was stupid!" with
"I'll be glad to listen to YOUR idea."

"You're weird!" with
"It helps me to come up with great ideas."

"Rolled eyes..."
with a big **SMILE**!!!

The WagiLabs kids in Charlottesville, Virginia helped a mom and two young daughters start a "safe space" coffee shop. It's called **"Kindness Cafe"** and they employ people with disabilities to show that everyone is welcome.

Remember the game, "Simon says?" The WagiKids changed the name to "Kindness says..." to encourage coffee drinkers to think up fun things to do that are "kind." For example, show a smile, open a door, give a hug, or buy someone a coffee.

1. What ideas does the Kindness Cafe give you for your community?

2. How can the "Kindness says..." game be used in WagiLabs and in your school?

Understand Roles and Goals

Roles to Play and Duties to Perform

Capt. Wagi and his crew are daring, adventurous, and willing to set forth into uncharted territories to create ideas for good. They are all entrepreneurs who take risks and are eager to travel to the ends of the earth to help solve community challenges.

The crew are all willing to live by the WagiWays, commit to the voyage, and pull their share of the load. Each crew member has a specific role to play and a set of duties to perform.

1. The **Captain** is elected by the crew and has the most authority aboard ship. Captains are even-tempered and neither too aggressive nor too meek.

2. The **Navigator** can use the stars to determine a ship's latitude and, therefore, can sail from east to west with reasonable ease. Figuring out longitude, however, is much harder, so sailing north to south involves instrumentation.

3. The **Quartermaster** handles the day-to-day operations of the ship. They are also in charge of discipline.

4. The **Boatswain**, or **Bosun**, leads shore parties to restock supplies or find material for repairs. They oversee activities such as dropping and weighing the anchor, setting the sails, and making sure the deck is swabbed.

5. The **Musicians** are popular onboard ships because ships spend weeks at sea. Musicians help pass the time and are

playing music while others are working.

6. The **Mates** outfit the ship with ropes, pulleys, sails, and other rigging as needed.

During a WagiLabs team exercise, everyone will choose their role for the exercise. You pick your role by writing the names Captain, Navigator, Quartermaster, Bosun, Musician, and Mate on piece of papers and mixing them up in a hat. Then you pick your role out of the hat.

1. The **Captain** is the leader of your exercise and makes sure we are following the WagiWays and saying, "Yes, **AND**..."

2. The **Navigator** is the timekeeper.

3. The **Quartermaster** takes all of the notes and handles any disruption.

4. The **Bosun** makes sure the team has all the needed supplies for the exercise.

5. The **Musician** is the fun keeper and in charge of music.

6. The **Mates** are the helpers throughout the exercise.

After the exercise is completed, everyone disembarks from the voyage. You will take on new roles by drawing from the hat again, at the start of the next team exercise.

How Do We Come Up with Ideas?

The I.D.E.A.S. Process!

At WagiLabs, we are all about ideas for good. So we created an idea process you can remember.

Let's walk through the process so you can follow it on our WagiVoyage and during the exercises.

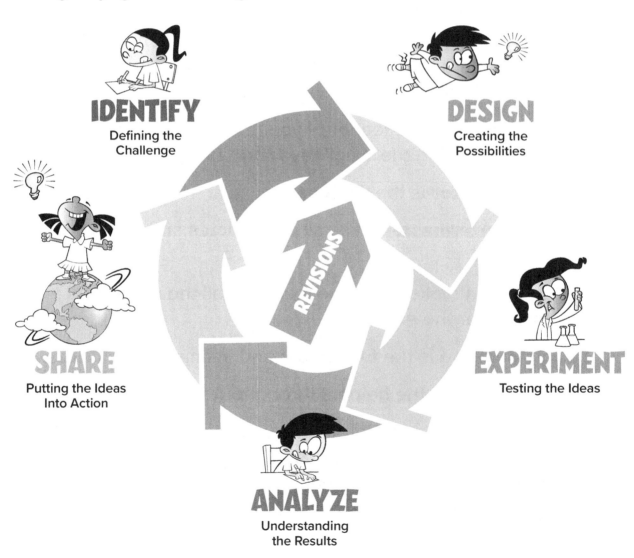

IDENTIFY
Defining the Challenge

DESIGN
Creating the Possibilities

SHARE
Putting the Ideas Into Action

REVISIONS

EXPERIMENT
Testing the Ideas

ANALYZE
Understanding the Results

IDENTIFY

To build a home, an architect speaks to the client about their needs: **how** many bedrooms and bathrooms?

To make a cake, a baker talks to the customer about their needs: **what** flavor and **how** should it be decorated?

When you are trying to solve a challenge, the five "W" questions (**What, Why, Who, When**, and **Where**) will help you define your challenge. You will learn more about these five questions starting on page 69.

DESIGN

Now you get to become a brainstormer and create exciting ideas to fill the needs we have uncovered and defined. No idea is too big or too small. You will learn about brainstorming on page 77.

EXPERIMENT

Now that you have ideas, it's time to experiment with possible solutions by building models or prototypes and testing them.

Some prototypes, such as sketches or storyboards, show what your idea looks like. Others, like mock-ups or models, demonstrate how your idea works. You will learn about creating prototypes starting on page 98.

ANALYZE

Effective experiments require you to analyze information, evaluate your design, reflect on your thinking, and propose revisions to improve your ideas. All of these skills are vital to becoming a critical thinker.

It's fine to let go of some ideas and create something new! In the idea world, letting go of an idea is called "**pivoting**."

SHARE

Sharing what you have learned in WagiLabs is called "Playing It Forward." It's one way to spread the word about doing good — so more kids help more people!

While sailing on our voyage, we will be using **science**, **technology**, **engineering**, and **mathematics** to chart our course. These four components of our trip are what we call **STEM.**

We have **STEM** exercises through out our PlayBook. The goals of the exercises are to encourage:

1. team building

2. questioning and brainstorming

3. learning from trial and error and

4. celebrating success.

On the next page is your first exercise. The goal of this exercise is to learn how to work together and have fun!

Marshmallow/Spaghetti Challenge

Challenge:

Build one free-standing structure with a marshmallow on top using no more than twenty sticks of spaghetti, one yard of tape, one yard of string, and one marshmallow.

The RULES:

1. The structure is measured from the tabletop surface to the top of the marshmallow. That means the structure cannot be suspended from a higher structure, like a chair, ceiling, or chandelier.

2. The entire marshmallow needs to be on the top of the structure. Cutting or eating part of the marshmallow disqualifies the team.

3. Teams can use as many or as few of the twenty spaghetti sticks, as much or as little of the string or tape.

4. Teams can break the spaghetti and cut the tape and string.

5. Teams cannot hold on to the structure after time runs out.

Trial One:

Build the structure in just **five minutes**.

After building, measure the height of your structure and test if it will support the weight of one marshmallow? The marshmallow must sit firmly on top of your structure.

Take photos of your structure and debrief the success or failure of your design and building process.

Then come up with three guidelines for building a more successful structure in the future.

1.

2.

3.

Trial Two:

Using your new guidelines, build another free-standing structure with a marshmallow on top in **fifteen minutes**.

After building, measure the height of your structure and test if it will support the weight of one marshmallow? The marshmallow must sit firmly on top of your structure. Take photos of your structure and debrief the success or failure of your design and building process.

Come up with an additional three guidelines for building a successful structure in the future.

1.

2.

3.

Compare the results from your two building projects.

1. Were both building attempts successful?

2. Which building attempt was taller?

3. Which building attempt used less materials?

4. What building techniques made the tower stronger?

5. Does the size of the base alter the strength of the tower?

6. How do you think you worked as a group?

Your Journal

Quietly reflect on your activities today. What did you discover about yourself? Write. Draw. Doodle.

"Stop and Pop!"

Hey, it's Wagi here!

I Can!

In a couple minutes you are going to learn the WagiCheer. I believe in the power of positive thinking — and most of the time, I'm pretty good at it!

But, I have to admit that I can't always control the thought balloons flying around my head. Sometimes, the negative ones get in my way. Like when I'm trying to solve a challenge, and nothing is working, my thought balloons can say...

Give up... it will never work!

I'm not good at anything!

If I follow my bad thoughts and give up, I feel sad or frustrated because I don't solve the problem. That's called having a "self-fulfilling" thought. When I think something won't work and give up — BLAMMO! It doesn't work.

So, how do I get rid of these annoying, self-defeating thoughts and turn them into positive thoughts?

I "POP" the negative thought balloons using my smile and my breath. When my negative doubts disappear, I feel better, and I think of a positive thought like "**I can do it.**"

Then I come up with new ideas — and find out I can solve the problem after all! It sounds weird, but it works! Try it for yourself.

Anytime a bad thought makes you doubt yourself or think about quitting ...

1. First, put a big smile on your face.

2. Then slow down your breathing and take three, long breaths in and out ... in and out ... in and out.

3. Observe your body as you start to feel calmer.

4. "POP!" Watch those self-defeating thought balloons disappear into thin air and put in a positive thought.

And hopefully, you'll feel better, happier, and ready to take the next steps forward!

Learning to recognize your feelings and calm your thoughts is called Mindfulness. It takes practice — a lot of practice. To help you remember my popping technique, I made this STOP sign.

S stands for: **Smile**

T stands for: **Tak**e three slow in and out breaths

O stands for: **Observe** your body and feelings

P stands for: **Pop** those negative thoughts

Now, as we embark on our WagiLabs journey together, if you ever hear little negative thoughts in your head saying, "Give up!" or "Don't trust your ideas!" hold up that sign and STOP them!

Don't worry; if you need help, I'll always be by your side! So watch for my little **Mindfulness Thought Balloons** to help you stay focused on achieving big ideas for your community and the world!

STOP
and
Smile

The WagiCheer!

Wagi created a team cheer to help us remember the "WagiWays" as we dive into our journey to make the world better. The cheer is our kids' promise that we'll share our ideas, play, and work together, and follow our passions to make our ideas happen!

Chant the cheer as you act out each step.

Wonder

 (Arms out, palms up)

Yes, AND

(High-five)

Get Messy

 (Both arms circle up and out in front of body)

I Can!

(Fist pump)

Wagi!

(Super hero pose)

You are now entering the

Sea of Curiosity!

Your mission will be to:

☐ Discover Our Passions

What are your passions? Which passions do you share with others? In WagiLabs, asking curious questions will help us discover our passions and identify the things we love to do.

☐ Be a Detective

WagiLabs is all about coming up with ideas to make life better. Before we can help people, let's do some investigation to see what people need.

☐ Uncover Needs

When are people unhappy? You guessed it! When they don't have the things they need, face dangers in their community, or don't feel safe. Time for more detective work!

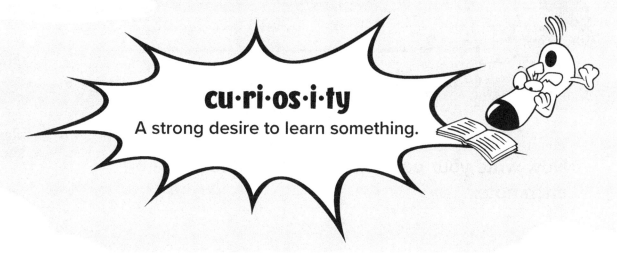

cu·ri·os·i·ty
A strong desire to learn something.

Discover Our Passions!

Curiosity is a strong desire to know or learn something. What is Wagi, our mascot, most excited to learn about?

How to catch a flying Frisbee. How to dig a better hole. How to scare a cat. Name four more fun activities that Wagi enjoys:

_____   _____

_____   _____

Now, think about what excites you — your passions. Do you like sports, animals, music or drawing? How about helping others? What do you like to do more than anything else?

Write down three things that make you happy every time you do or think about them. These are your passions.

1. _____

2. _____

3. _____

video games

music

playing soccer

Now write your passions on sticky notes, one on each note.

When everyone is ready, organize your sticky notes on the wall in three categories: Do with friends, do with family, and do by yourself.

Look at all of the sticky notes. Which passions are your favorites? Have each person put three blue dots on their favorite passion, two blue dots on the second favorite, and one blue dot on the third favorite.

When everyone has voted, count up how many dots each passion has received. Then make a "Top 10" list of kid passions, and read them out loud.

Our "Top 10" Kid Passions

1. _____

2. _____

3. _____

4. _____

5. _____

6. _____

7. _____

8. _____

9. _____

10. _____

We all see things in our own special way. In WagiLabs, our passions help us come up with ideas, work together, and choose the jobs that we do best.

We're going to be a great team!

Chasing Your Dreams

The Life of a Kidpreneur

Do you know what it's like to play fetch with our dog, Wagi?

You throw the ball and Wagi takes off after it like a rocket ship to the stars.

Wagi is **focused.**

Wagi is **determined.**

Wagi is **unstoppable.**

When he finally gets the ball, he won't let go until you throw it again.

Kidpreneurs like you are a lot like Wagi. They chase their ideas with **determination.**

They are determined when they're solving an important challenge.

They work hard, try new things, and make mistakes while developing their ideas.

Kidpreneurs get **messy!**

Kidpreneurs keep going until they reach their goals.

Then they celebrate and feel great about their accomplishments.

It feels good to **"wag"** your tail!

WagiLabs
IDEAS FOR GOOD!

www.wagilabs.org

Characteristics of a Kidpreneur:

Read "Chasing Your Dreams" comic strip on page 28. Can you identify the characteristics of a Kidpreneur? Write them in a list.

Top Characteristics of a Kidpreneur

☐ _____

☐ _____

☐ _____

☐ _____

☐ _____

☐ _____

☐ _____

☐ _____

☐ _____

☐ _____

Make a check in the box next to each characteristic that matches you. Then, look at the unchecked boxes. They show important areas to work on at WagiLabs to become a successful Kidpreneur.

Your "Brain/Body" Dominances

Your Experiment:

Let's take a trip from your eyes to your feet to determine the brain/body dominance of your body. Below is a chart to fill in your responses.

Brain/Body Dominance

Left Side of Body		Right Side of Body
☐	Eyes	☐
☐	Wink	☐
☐	Smile	☐
☐	Arms	☐
☐	Thumbs	☐
☐	Hands	☐
☐	Crossing Legs	☐
☐	Feet	☐
☐	Thoughts	☐
☐	Visualization	☐
☐		☐
Creative Right Side of Brain		Analytical Left Side of Brain

Eyes

Most think we focus on an object with both our eyes. Actually, we use just one eye to focus on what we're doing or reading. To determine which eye is dominant, simply hold your thumb at arm's length out in front of you and use your thumb to block out a small object on a far wall, such as a light switch or corner of a picture frame.

Do this with both eyes open. When the light switch is blocked out, then close your right eye. If your thumb is still blocking out the light switch, it was your left eye that was dominant in focusing. If the light switch "moved," then you focused on it with your right eye.

Determining which eye is dominant has become very beneficial for athletes.

1. How would your eye dominance help or hurt an athlete's performance?

2. If their eye dominance hurts the athlete's ability, how do they compensate to neutralize the eye dominance?

Wink

Wink one eye, then the other. Does one feel more natural to wink? If so, that's your dominant eye for winking. Mark down your dominance.

Why do most people wink their non-dominant eye?

Smile

Smile at yourself while looking in a mirror. Which side of your mouth goes higher? If you can't tell, look for which side of your face has more wrinkles. The higher, more wrinkled side is your dominant one. Mark down your dominance.

Arms

Cross your arms with one arm on top of the other. Whichever arm is on top is your dominant arm. Mark down your dominance.

Thumbs

Bring your hands together, interlocking your fingers, making sure you have one thumb on top of the other. Whichever thumb is on top is your dominant thumb. Now, separate your hands and bring them back together with the other thumb on top. Feels awkward, doesn't it? Mark down your dominance.

Hands

Mark down which hand you use for writing. If you were switched in grade school from left to right, you are still considered left-handed for this exercise. Try writing your name with your non-dominant hand.

Legs

Cross your legs at the knee. Which leg feels more comfortable on top? That's your dominant leg—mark it down.

Feet

If I rolled a ball to you, which foot would you use to kick it? That's your dominant foot—mark it down.

What sports would benefit from you being able to use both feet equally well for kicking?

Thoughts

This exercise will require help from another person. Ask a friend to ask you several questions in a row and observe your eye movements.

1. Have them ask a question that requires calculation of an answer?

2. Have them ask a question that requires visualization of a situation?

3. Have them ask a question that makes you feel a little sad?

4. Have them ask a question that is fun and makes you laugh?

Do not have the friend stare at you because you'll stare back. Your eyes need to be relaxed to move.

Have your friend tell you if your eyes moved to the right or the left, up or down or a combination of moves. Mark down the results in the below table.

Eye Movement Data Table

QUESTIONS	UP	DOWN	LEFT	RIGHT	No Movement
Calculation					
Visulization					
Sad					
Fun					
		TOTAL			

Total your left and right eye movements. Mark down the side that has the most movements on the Brain/Body Dominance chart on page 30.

Visualization

Close your eyes. Now visualize a circular wall clock on the wall in front of you. In your mind, reach out and take the clock off the wall and put it in front of your face. Now put one finger of one hand at twelve o'clock and one finger of the other hand at three o'clock. Open your eyes and note if three o'clock is on the right or left side of your face; mark down which side.

If you saw the clock both ways on your face or if neither leg feels more or less comfortable when crossed on top of the other, then your dominance for that part of your body is mixed. On the chart, you can check both the right and left sides.

Scoring Your Dominances

Count up the number of left and right-side dominances. The usual score is seven for the right side and three for the left. These body dominances then show the exact opposite brain dominance, because the left side of the body is controlled by the right side of the brain and vice versa. So, if your body score is seven right-side and three left, then your brain dominance profile is seven left-side and three right.

Becoming Unstuck

Knowing your brain/body dominances can help you when you feel "stuck" trying to write a report or make a tough decision. By using your non-dominant side you can "jump-start" your brain. It's like adding new batteries to your flashlight.

Here are my favorite jump-starts:

1. Cross your arms or legs in the nondominant way.

2. Write or use your mouse with your other hand.

3. When you're looking at a magazine, instead of browsing through the pages from left to right, browse the pages from right to left.

4. Watch a TV show or listen to a song you would never pick.

5. Sit in a different seat at school, the library or at dinner.

Have fun!!!

Your Favorites

Knowing what others like can help build our team. We all don't need to like the same things to be great teammates. In fact, liking different things can help us decide the roles we play as future detectives. Please list your favorite:

Animal _____

Athlete _____

Book _____

Candy _____

Cereal _____

Color _____

Drink _____

Hat _____

Junk Food _____

Movie _____

Musical Instrument _____

Restaurant _____

Song _____

Sport _____

Sports Team _____

Subject in School _____

Super Hero _____

Video Game _____

Your Journal

Quietly reflect on your activities today. What did you discover about yourself? Write. Draw. Doodle.

Now it's time for the
WagiCheer!
See page 24

Be a Detective!

A detective's job is to find information about someone or something. Detectives do this by being good observers, asking good questions, and taking a lot of notes.

At WagiLabs, we want to find information about ways to make life better. The best place to start exploring what people need is in our community, so we can help people we know.

The drawing on the next page shows the KidpreneurShip and Wagi's seaworthy community. Practice your detective skills by looking closely at the ship, the water, and the sky asking the following questions:

1. What do you think life is like in onboard the ship?

2. What is the best thing?

3. What is the hardest thing?

4. What would make life better?

5. What would you change?

Map It!

Now draw a map that shows your community and the places you visit like school, stores, churches and parks. You can be traveling by walking, riding, or driving.

Take fifteen minutes to draw your map on the following page. You can write labels and draw pictures. When time's up, share your maps with everyone.

You can also take pictures of your community and go online to find a Google Maps view of your area.

Detective Questions:

Choose partners to create teams, and then use the maps to do detective work in your neighborhoods.

Here's the same list of detective questions to help you learn more about your community.

1. What is life like in your community?

2. What is the best thing?

3. What is the hardest thing? What obstacles do you see?

4. What would make life better?

5. What would you change?

Draw a Map of your Community

Finally, write your team answers into a "Best Things" versus "Challenges" list for your community.

Our Community

Best Things   vs.   **Challenges**

_____   _____

_____   _____

_____   _____

_____   _____

_____   _____

_____   _____

_____   _____

_____   _____

_____   _____

_____   _____

Wink & Snap

1. Try winking one eye and snapping the fingers on your opposite hand.

2. Then wink your other eye and snap the fingers on your other hand.

3. Switch back and forth and try to go faster.

This exercise will wake up your brain because you are doing two different things at once and using opposite sides of your body.

Your Journal

Quietly reflect on your activities today. What did you discover about yourself? Write. Draw. Doodle.

Now it's time for the
WagiCheer!
See page 24

Uncover Needs!

When we explored our community, we used our detective skills to find both the best things and the challenges.

The best things make people happy. What makes people unhappy? In many places, people are unhappy because they can't get the things they need to stay healthy and feel safe.

These things are called "basic needs." Imagine being stranded on a desert island. What would your basic needs be? What would you need to survive?

Make a list.

1. _____

2. _____

3. _____

4. _____

5. _____

6. _____

7. _____

8. _____

"Smash-Up!" Exercise:

Now that we have thought about basic needs, let's play a game called "Smash-Up." There are three categories — Places, Challenges, and Basic Needs — and six items in each category. Mixing and matching category items can help us think of new ideas and identify our community's needs.

PLACES	CHALLENGES	BASIC NEEDS
1. School	1. Accidents	1. Food
2. Home	2. Trash	2. Shelter
3. Park	3. Crime	3. Water
4. Market	4. Bullying	4. Clothing
5. Street	5. Germs	5. Safety
6. Gym	6. Low Income	6. Good Health

How to Play: Split your group into teams.

1. Have each team roll a die three times (or pick three numbers out of a box).

2. Choose the **Place** that matches the first number, the **Challenge** that matches the second number, and the **Need** that matches the third number.

3. Write your picks in the blanks of the Challenge Sentence on the next page.

4. Then brainstorm situations that might be caused by your Smash-Up!

Here's an Example:

Let's say our numbers are: **1**, **5**, **6**. Our Smash-Up would be:

PLACE = School

CHALLENGE = Germs

NEED = Good Health

We'd write our three picks in the Challenge Sentence, like this:

In a _____ School _____ , how can _____ Germs _____
(PLACE)   (CHALLENGE)

cause problems with _____ Good Health _____ , or keep people
(NEEDS)

from getting the _____ Good Health _____ they need?
(NEEDS)

Then, as a group, we can ask ourselves the five "**W**" questions regarding the School/Germs/Good Health Smash-Up challenge.

- **What** kind of germs are they?

- **Why** do germs cause you to get sick?

- **Who** is most affected by these germs?

- **When** do the germs spread?

- **Where** in the school do the germs appear?

To get more insight into germ transmission we will now conduct our second **STEM** exercise.

This exercise will help us understand how germs are transmitted and what steps we can take to prevent the transmission.

What Form of "Hand Greeting" Transfers the Most Germs?

Your Experiment:

Imagine it is flu season at your school, and the school nurse asked your team to research ideas on how to reduce the spread of flu germs.

You divide your experiment into four stages. First, determining the spread by hand transmission, second by air transmission, third by surface transmission, and finally, you come up with prevention techniques.

1. Hand Transmission

1. Put one tsp. of flour or corn starch on three kids' hands. Have those three kids shake hands with three other kids, who then shake hands with three other kids, who then shake hands with three other kids. After the handshaking, count how many kids have flour on their hands? Describe what parts of your hands show the flour. Take pictures of your hands.

2. Now everyone washes their hands with soap and water.

3. Now that you've seen how easily germs can spread through a handshake, it's time to identify the specific problem that we are trying to solve with the upcoming experiment. Fill in the blanks to state the problem:

   Which way of greeting others _____ the _____ amount of _____?

4. Brainstorm additional ways kids can greet each other during flu season. Look at your brainstormed ideas, do you have some guesses as to what are the healthiest ways to greet someone?

5. Repeat step one of this exercise with each way you thought kids could greet each other. Please take pictures. Wash your hands with soap and water between hand greetings.

6. Create a chart to demonstrate which method of hand greeting transferred the most flour or corn starch. Show the areas of the hands that had the most build-up of flour or corn starch.

Questions to Answer:

What could this mean for the spread of germs?

Does it make a difference if you are right-handed or left-handed when spreading germs?

Could replacing the handshake with another form of hand greeting during flu season reduce the spread of germs?

2. Air Transmission

1. Place a piece of tape on the floor to make a starting line. Place pieces of tape at 1, 2, 3, 4, 5, and 6 feet from the starting point.

2. Stand at the starting point and hold a spray bottle of water at your mouth level, pointing away from your body.

3. Have your friend stand on the tape that is 6 feet away from the starting point and hold a piece of black construction paper up in front of their face.

4. Spray the spray bottle one time to simulate a sneeze. Your friend should quickly look at the paper and use a white crayon to mark the general outline of where the water hit on the paper.

5. Repeat these steps with a new piece of black paper from the 5, 4, 3, 2, and 1-foot lines.

6. Make a graph that compares the "sneeze" areas for the assigned distances.

3. Surface Transmission

1. Make a list of at least ten things you touch every day like phone, doorknobs, tv remote, etc.

2. Now put some flour in the palm of your hand. Then touch the items on your list. Wash your hands after touching each item and reapply the flour or corn starch.

3. Where does the flour or corn starch spread?

4. How far did the flour or corn starch travel?

Questions to Answer:

What could this mean for the spreading of germs?

Could this mean that daily cleaning of these items is an effective method of disease prevention?

4. Prevention Strategies

What are three things you can do to prevent spreading germs?

1.

2.

3.

One of the most important preventive solution is to wash your hands with soap and water for twenty seconds. The majority of kids say that they wash their hands after using a restroom.

In reality, only 50% of kids in school wash their hands. Only 33% of females and 8% of males use soap when washing hands. Globally, handwashing after using the restroom is only 19%.

Washing hands with soap helps prevent infections because:

1. People frequently touch their eyes, nose, and mouth without

realizing it. Germs can get into the body through the eyes, nose, and mouth and make us sick.

2. Germs from unwashed hands can get into foods and drinks while people prepare or consume them. Bacteria can multiply in foods or beverages and make us sick.

3. Germs from unwashed hands can be transferred to other objects, like handrails, tabletops, or toys, and then moved to another person's hands and make us sick.

Questions to Answer:

What can we do to get more people to wash their hands with soap and water for twenty seconds?

1.

2.

3.

How do you know when you have washed for twenty seconds? **Sing a song** that lasts about twenty seconds.

If soap and water are not available, what can you do?

1.

2.

3.

One convenient idea is to use an 70% alcohol-based hand sanitizer. Rub the gel over all the surfaces of your hands and fingers until your hands are dry. This gel application should take around twenty seconds, so sing your song!

Now it's time to get back to identifying our community need and writing a challenge statement.

Your First Community Smash-Up!

Now, play Smash-Up using the Places, Challenges, and Basic Needs you discovered doing detective work in your community.

To start, add information to all three columns.

PLACES	CHALLENGES	BASIC NEEDS
1.	1.	1.
2.	2.	2.
3.	3.	3.
4.	4.	4.
5.	5.	5.
6.	6.	6.

To play, roll the die three times, and fill in the blanks.

Your community Smash-Up is:

PLACE = _____

CHALLENGE = _____

NEED = _____

Write your three picks in the Challenge Sentence:

In a _____ , how can _____
                (PLACE)   (CHALLENGE)

cause problems with _____ , or keep people
                              (NEEDS)

from getting the _____ they need?
                          (NEEDS)

Together, brainstorm some situations that might be caused by your Smash-Up.

Imagine yourself in the place you picked. Think about the need and brainstorm how the problem might cause some challenging situations. To come up with ideas, fill in the blanks in these questions, and ask yourselves:

Where in the _____ did the problem happen?
                    (PLACE)

What kind of _____ might happen in this place?
                        (CHALLENGE)

What _____ might be involved?
        (NEEDS)

Who would be affected by the _____?
                                          (CHALLENGE)

Your Second Community Smash-Up!

Let's use your detective lists to play again!

Roll the die three more times, and then fill in the blanks.

This time, your community Smash-Up is:

PLACE = _____

CHALLENGE = _____

NEED = _____

Add your three picks into the new sentence:

In a _____ , how can _____
(PLACE)   (CHALLENGE)

cause problems with _____ , or keep people
                                      (NEEDS)

from getting the _____ they need?
                            (NEEDS)

Together, brainstorm some situations that might be caused by your Smash-Up.

Imagine yourself in the place you picked. Think about the need and brainstorm how the problem might cause some challenging situations. To come up with ideas, fill in the blanks in these questions, and ask yourselves:

Where in the _____ did the problem happen?
                    (PLACE)

What kind of _____ might happen in this place?
                      (CHALLENGE)

What _____ might be involved?
        (NEEDS)

Who would be affected by the _____?
                                      (CHALLENGE)

Create a Community Needs List:

After you finish brainstorming, create a list of the needs you discovered in our community.

Our Community Needs

1. _____

2. _____

3. _____

4. _____

5. _____

6. _____

7. _____

8. _____

Now, have each team member decide which needs they think are most important; and put three dots on the most important need, two dots on second most important need, and one dot on the third most important need.

When everyone has voted, count the dots and select the top community need. Write this need in the box below.

Top Community Need

Now, ask yourselves: Which people in our community have this need?

Person _____

Person _____

Person _____

Imagine what it is like to be someone on your list, so you can better understand how they feel.

Please take five minutes to talk with your teammates about how the person facing this situation would describe the need or tell others about it.

Write down your ideas.

1.

2.

3.

To give you more ideas about your community needs, pretend that you are another person on your list. How do you think that person feels about his or her situation?

We like to say that trying to imagine what other people feel is like walking in their shoes. At the next destination on our WagiJourney, the Island of Compassion, we are going to learn more about walking in others' shoes and having empathy.

Having empathy is how we understand the changes needed in the world.

Mindful Moment

Scan Your Body

As a detective, you scanned your community to uncover challenges. Did you know that you can use the same Observation skills to scan your body and uncover physical challenges such as stress and tension?

It only takes a moment! Here's what you have to do.

Start at the top of your head and, as you breathe, notice how your body feels. Move your focus from your head to your neck, shoulders, chest, stomach, arms, hands, legs, all the way down to the tip of your toes.

If you find that any part of your body feels tense, take an extra breath, and relax that part.

When your body scan is over, you will feel calmer, and your brain will be ready to focus again on your latest project.

Your Journal

Quietly reflect on your activities today. What did you discover about yourself? Write. Draw. Doodle.

Now it's time for the
WagiCheer!
See page 24

Arriving at the

Island of Compassion!

Your mission will be to:

☐ Walk in Others' Shoes

By walking in other people's shoes, we can see life as they see it, and feel what they feel. That is called having compassion.

☐ Define the Challenge

Defining a challenge means thinking about challenges and goals of the person's shoes you walked in.

☐ Brainstorm Solutions

Everyone gets to share lots of ideas — and no one says "**NO!**" We see what's **good** about our ideas, and that helps us come up with even more compassionate ideas!

☐ Get Feedback

Feedback helps improve our ideas and builds our confidence to make our ideas a reality.

Compassion

com·pas·sion
A concern for the struggles and misfortunes of others.

Walk in Others' Shoes!

Part 1: Imagine

Today we're going to think about a skill that can help us give others what they need. It's called **empathy**.

When you have empathy, you can "put yourself in someone else's shoes" to see what they see and feel what they feel. When you learn from empathy and help the other person it's called having **compassion**.

Have you ever hurt your foot and had to use crutches? Suddenly, your favorite shoe doesn't fit, and you have to wear a cast when you walk. How does life change when one shoe changes?

1. You might feel lopsided or off-balance with a shoe on one foot and a big cast on the other.

2. You might have trouble getting out of bed, taking a shower, or getting dressed.

3. It might be hard to walk, climb stairs, run on the playground, or keep up with your friends.

Once a cast comes off, most people can run and jump and play just like before. But what if your cast never comes off? What if you had to live with a broken leg for the rest of your life?

Do you know anyone who has a disability? This person might have a leg, arm, or back that doesn't work well or who uses a wheelchair? Close your eyes for a minute and imagine what that person's life is like.

Part 2: Act It Out

People who are disabled or older might have any of the physical limits we just talked about. Can you imagine what it would be like to live their lives? How would you feel?

Use one of the props on the list to explore what life might be like when you are very old. Be careful! Have your team members help you.

Then try on the next prop until you have tried all five. As you are wearings the props, try to do different things to help you imagine situations you might face each day.

☐ Walk with one foot in a bucket to simulate having an injured foot

☐ Wear jelly-covered glasses to simulate having poor vision

☐ Wear a sling to simulate having a non-functioning arm

☐ Wear a weighted backpack to simulate having a back or movement problem

☐ Wear oversized gloves to simulate having problems with your hands and fingers

A Day in the Life

Waking Up

Sleeping

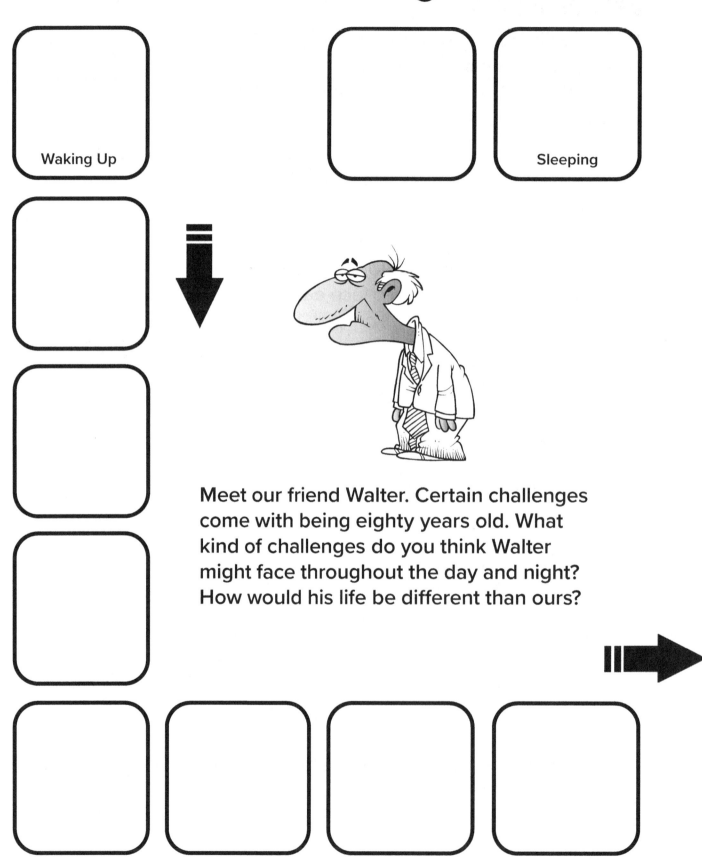

Meet our friend Walter. Certain challenges come with being eighty years old. What kind of challenges do you think Walter might face throughout the day and night? How would his life be different than ours?

# of Walter!

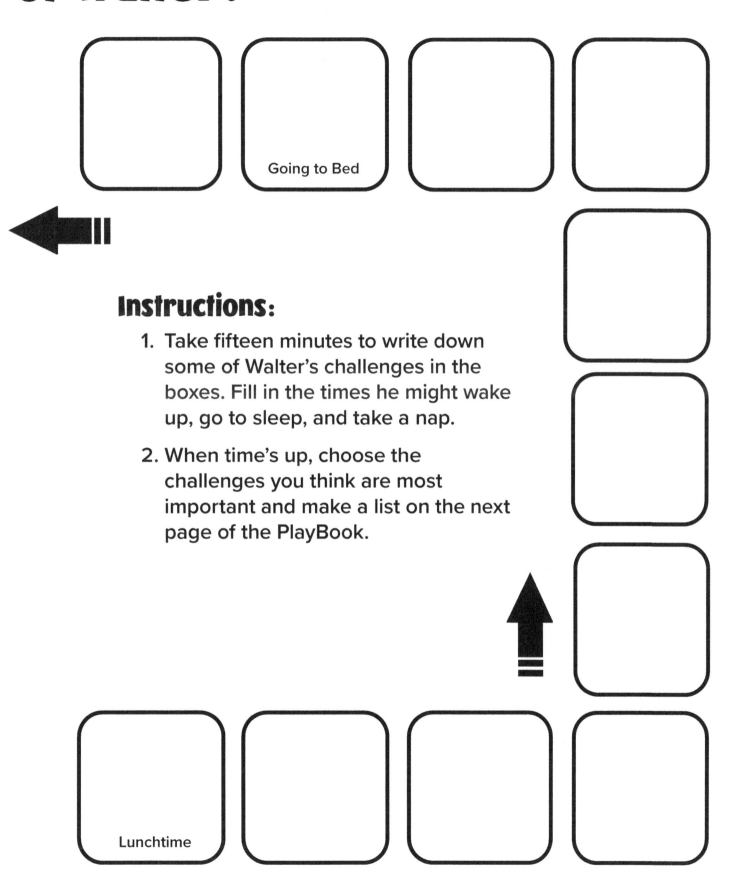

Going to Bed

Instructions:

1. Take fifteen minutes to write down some of Walter's challenges in the boxes. Fill in the times he might wake up, go to sleep, and take a nap.

2. When time's up, choose the challenges you think are most important and make a list on the next page of the PlayBook.

Lunchtime

Part 3: From First Steps to Next Steps

Look at your "Day in the Life" ideas and make a list of the top five challenges people like Walter face.

1.

2.

3.

4.

5.

Part 4: Let's Get Creative!!!

Athletes have special shoes to help them move easily and do their best. Why don't we invent a WagiShoe to help elderly people move easily?

What would the shoe allow them to do? How would our WagiShoe be different from sneakers, boots, flip-flops, high-heels, foot casts and bare feet? Could it have superhero powers?

1.

2.

3.

4.

5.

Part 5: Draw a Picture of Your Shoe for Walter!

Label the parts that have special features or powers.

A Day in the Life of

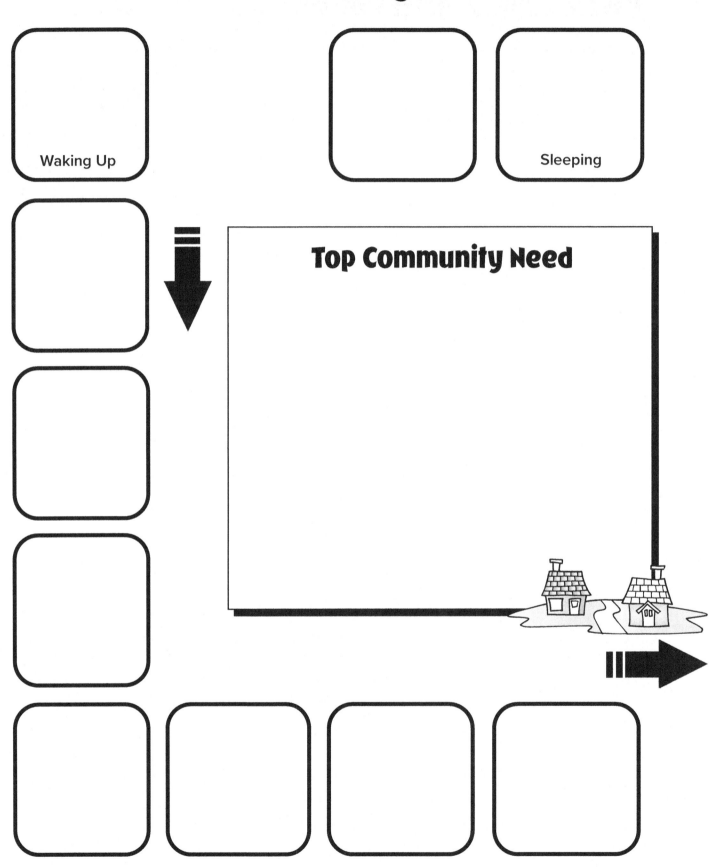

Waking Up

Sleeping

Top Community Need

Your Top Community Need!

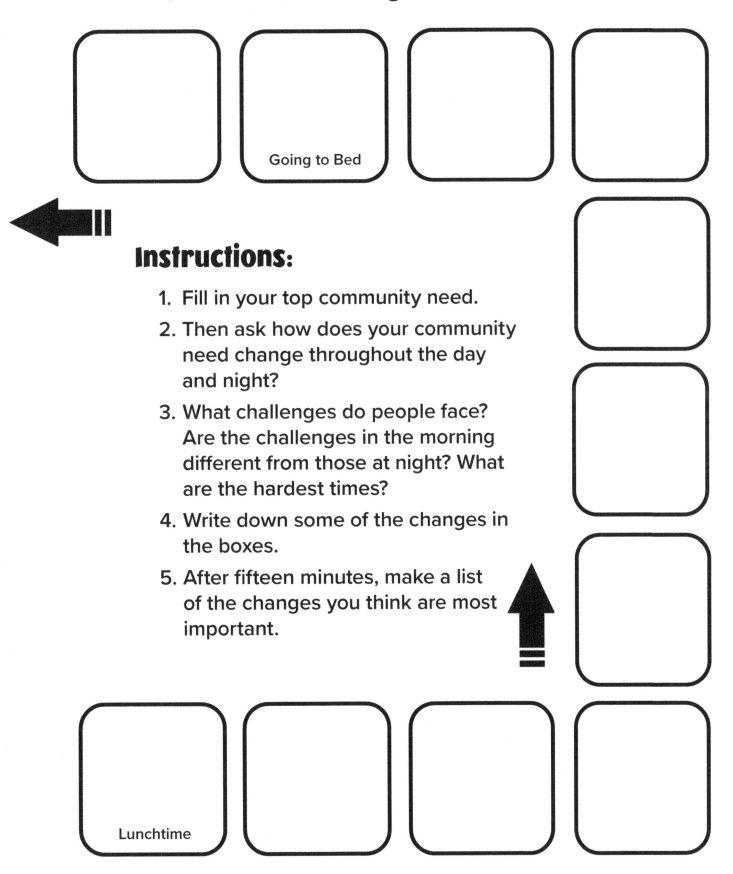

Going to Bed

Instructions:

1. Fill in your top community need.

2. Then ask how does your community need change throughout the day and night?

3. What challenges do people face? Are the challenges in the morning different from those at night? What are the hardest times?

4. Write down some of the changes in the boxes.

5. After fifteen minutes, make a list of the changes you think are most important.

Lunchtime

Part 6: Insights From Day in the Life

List five important things you learned from your "Day in the Life" exercise about your community needs.

1.

2.

3.

4.

5.

Show Us Your #UnSelfie

"How can you use a smartphone to **'do good'** in your community?"

A "Selfie" is a self-portrait photograph, usually taken at arm's length to emphasize certain body features as attractively as possible.

What if you took "UnSelfie" photographs or video to emphasize the **best thing**s and the **challenges** in your community?

We know you can come up with great ideas to improve your community, and we want to help you make them happen!

Send us your "UnSelfies" and our WagiLabs team will help you brainstorm ideas for your community.

woof@wagilabs.org

Your Journal

Quietly reflect on your activities today. What did you discover about yourself? Write. Draw. Doodle.

Now it's time for the

WagiCheer!

See page 24

Define the Challenge!

To find solutions for our top community need, we have first to define the challenge.

Begin with the End in Mind!

To build a home, a carpenter begins with blueprints. To make a cake, a baker starts with a recipe.

When you are trying to solve a challenge, thinking about your goal helps you create a plan. These five "W" questions will help you picture the future and write your challenge definition:

> "**WHAT** results do we want to achieve by solving our community challenge? **WHAT** is our goal, **WHAT** do people need?"

1.

2.

3.

"Why?" is the question kids most often ask. Kids ask "Why?" sixty five times per day. Now, here's a "Why" question for YOU to answer:

"WHY do we want to achieve the goal or result you just described for the first question? In what ways will life get better?"

1.

2.

3.

Then follow up with these questions:

"WHO has the need or is facing the challenge?"

1.

2.

3.

"WHEN does the challenge occur?"

1.

2.

3.

"**WHERE** does the challenge occur?"

1.

2.

3.

Now you can define your community challenge.

What + Why + Who + When + Where = Your Challenge Definition

Turn your answers to the "W" questions into a two to three sentence definition of your community challenge.

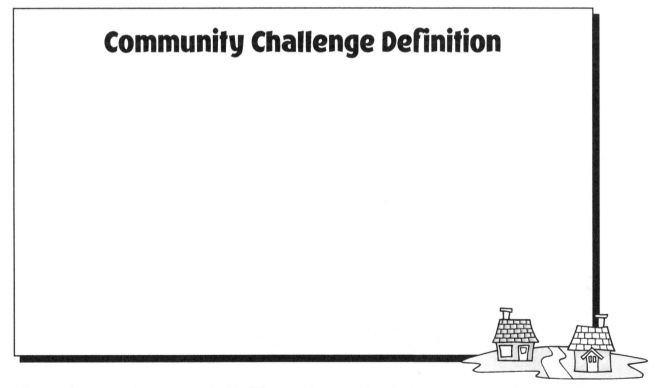

Community Challenge Definition

Now that we have a definition of our challenge, we are ready to brainstorm solutions.

Be More Buffalo?

Wagi was excited. He was reading about the buffalos in the Rocky Mountain area of the United States. There was a quote from the first female chief of the Cherokee American Indian Nation. It said:

"Whenever I'm confronted with a tough challenge, I do not prolong the torment, I become the buffalo."

"What does that mean, Wagi thought? I can't wait to read more and find out."

When storms come to Colorado, the storms usually start in the west and roll out toward the east. Cows sense the storm coming from the west and start to run toward the east. The only problem, cows aren't very fast and the storm catches up with them.

Without knowing any better, the cows continue to try to outrun the storm. Instead of outrunning it, they actually run along with it, maximizing the time they experience the storm.

Wagi found out that when buffalo sense a storm coming over the Rocky Mountains, they run directly into the storm. With the buffalo heading west and the storm heading east, the buffalo reduce their exposure to the bad weather and the storm passes them very quickly.

Buffalo seldom stand with their backs to the wind. They face the wind. With the thickest part of their coat being at the front and their massive head and shoulders to block the wind, this stance helps to protect their core temperature. So buffalos are designed to run into the storm.

Your Exercise:

Create a chart comparing the time cows spend in various storms versus buffalo.

1. How fast can cows run? How fast can buffalo run? How fast do storms travel in the plains of Colorado? Thunderstorms versus snow storms?

2. Sketch the aerodynamics of a buffalo versus a cow.

3. Are there other characteristics of the animals that help them make their instinctive response to a storm?

Wagi thought, "could storms be like challenges in **my** life?"

Think of three challenges you are facing, like writing a paper or giving a presentation, and write them down.

1.

2.

3.

Then ask yourself these questions:

1. Are you avoiding any of them?

2. Are you running away from any of them?

3. Are you hoping any of them will go away?

If so, why are you doing this?

Then ask, what would a buffalo do?

WagiKids Got Talent!

To help you remember the "What, Why, Who, When and Where" questions we created a Wagi theme song. Sing and dance our song. Feel free to change the lyrics. Put music to it. Record it and upload for the world to hear and see.

Wagi **What**,
Wagi **Why**,
Just throw your hands up in the sky.

Wagi **Where** and
When and **Who**,
Go show the world what you can do!

Come on everybody — the time is now,
Put your hearts and heads together,
and live out loud.

You got what it takes, and you got the moves,
You gonna create big ideas, and bring
your dreams to life!

Wagi **What**,
Wagi **Why**,
Just throw your hands up in the sky.

Wagi **Where** and
When and **Who**,
Go show the world what you can do!

Your Journal

Quietly reflect on your activities today. What did you discover about yourself? Write. Draw. Doodle.

Now it's time for the
WagiCheer!
See page 24

Count the Squares

Count the number of squares you see in the graphic. Remember, squares have four equal sides. Once you see one answer, look for a second answer.

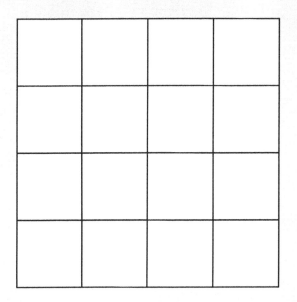

Your first answer: _____

Now, look for more: _____

Look one more time: _____

Your final answer: _____

What did you learn from these exercises that will help you create more ideas at WagiLabs?

Exercise answer is on the bottom of page 80, and please don't peek.

Brainstorm Solutions!

Last time, we learned how to describe a challenge and used What and Why questions to learn more about the challenges we chose.

We've been detectives uncovering needs and learned more about needs by walking in other people's shoes.

Now get ready to become brainstormers. Brainstormers create exciting ideas to fill the needs we have uncovered and defined.

What a Great Idea!

Have you ever heard the word "brainstorm?" What do you think it means?

When we "brainstorm," we let all our creative ideas flow out, like swirling winds in a storm. Brain–Storm, get it? No idea is too big or too small. Everyone gets to share lots of ideas.

To create a safe space for brainstorming, we throw out the old "rules of school." We reject rules like:

1. There is only one right answer.

2. The right answer is in the Teacher's Edition.

3. Don't pass notes.

4. The answer is not on the ceiling.

In brainstorming, the guidelines are:

1. Look for the second and third right answers.

2. The teacher or book doesn't give you the answer. You create the answer by thinking and asking questions.

3. Pass notes, collaborate, and appreciate different opinions.

4. The answers still aren't on the ceiling, but if you look with creative eyes, the questions might be.

Questions Brainstormers Ask:

We will ask these three questions in our brainstorms to find ideas to help solve our identified community challenge.

While brainstorming, when we hear any **new** idea, we say "Yes, **AND**" so we can let the possibilities of the idea dance in our head before we say anything negative. When you get an idea you like, you play with it.

What if this ... What if that ...

What if ... What if ...

Ideas need feedback to grow. It takes courage to share your idea with someone. When you do, most people want to help, so they say, "That's a cool idea!" Then they add one little word … "**BUUUUUT** …" and that's the kicker. That **BUT** — that **B-U-T** — means they want to tell you what they think is wrong with your brand new idea!

They might say:

> **But** … it's too hard to make!

> **But** … it'll cost too much!

> **But** … we don't have time to do that!

Sometimes, that little word "but" can stop you right in your tracks and make you say, "You're right, what a silly idea."

Is there a better way? You're doggone right there is! Just say "**AND**" instead. Say what's right about an idea before we look for what's wrong with it.

So, when I hear a new idea, I might say:

> Cool idea! "**AND**" it might help us solve this problem.

Saying "**AND**" lets you keep the door open and the ideas flowing. "**AND**" is a building block. It suggests that there are more ideas and possibilities out there. "**AND**" can also help you build bridges to get over problems with your idea.

> Awesome idea, "**AND**" it will make it less expensive.

> Great idea, "**AND**" we only have an hour to do it, so let's divide up the tasks.

So, WagiKids, as we move ahead on our journey, let's kick all those "**BUTS**" out of our language and build a mountain of problem-solving ideas with "**AND!**"

Brainstorming Guidelines

 Create a Safe Space

 Dream Big

 Say "Yes, AND ..." to all ideas.

 Be curious first, critical second.

 Come up with as many ideas as you can. Quantity counts!

 Build on the ideas of others.

 Encourage "wild" even impossible ideas.

 Do Good!

Exercise answer is (16 + 9 + 4 + 1 = 30).

Start Storming...

Step 1: Agree on Your Challenge

Turn back to page 71 and review your team's community challenge. Make sure you all agree on it. Write the challenge below so you can quickly refer to it.

Step 2: Think of Five "What if...?" Questions

What if ...? questions can help you come up with ideas to solve your challenge.

1. What if we did this ...

2. What if we changed this ...

3. What if everyone could ...

4. What if we had ...

5. What if we were given all of the money in the world ...

Make up your own What if ...? questions. It's fun to brainstorm!

Step 3: Now, Brainstorm Some Ideas

Ideas that are possible answers to your "What if ...?" questions.

1.

2.

3.

4.

5.

6.

7.

8.

9.

10.

Step 4. Identify the Strengths of Each Idea

For each idea, ask the team: "Why is it a good idea?" Think of ways each idea might help solve the community challenge.

1.

2.

3.

4.

5.

6.

7.

8.

9.

10.

Now, let's play the **Never** Game to see if it will help us come up with even more new ideas.

The Never Game!

"The sun rises, the sun sets.

Everything goes to its opposite.

Learn to see things, backwards, inside out, and upside down."

—Lao-Tzu

A **never** idea starts out as something you would **never** do. But, with a little help, it can turn into an amazing idea!

Let's play the **Never** Game to discover the magic of turning a **never** idea into a possibility for a great idea.

First, answer the question, then flip the answer into a possibility you might consider.

Where would I never want to go on vacation?

Now **FLIP** it ...

Tell why your **never** vacation spot might be a cool idea!

_____

_____

What would I never want to do today?

_____

Now **FLIP** it ...

Tell why your **never** activity might be a cool idea!

_____

_____

Did "flipping" your ideas generate any great ideas?

Was it fun?

Let's see if playing the **Never** Game can help us think of some unusual ways to solve our our community challenge.

Step 5. NeverNever Land

What would we never do
to solve our community challenge?

Never Do...

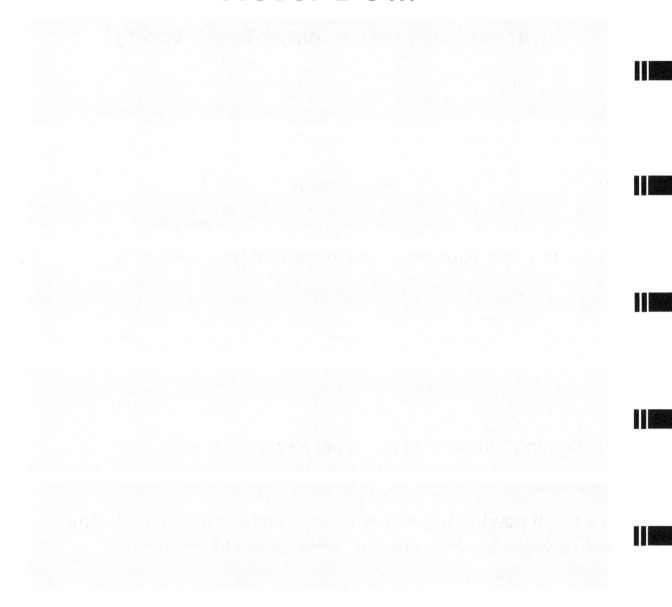

Have fun! Be **silly**!!!

Now, look at each one of your **never** ideas, and find a way to FLIP it ... to make it a great idea that can help solve our community challenge.

Idea Possibilities...

Congratulations, you completed your first brainstorm. Next, you'll show your ideas to other people to get their feedback. Their thoughts will help you decide which ideas to develop.

Before tackling a big brainstorm, you can use mindfulness to get your brain ready for the challenge.

You can use both your breath and your smile to show gratitude for your smart, adaptable brain.

When you take a breath in, say to yourself,

"I am calming my body with a smile."

When you breathe out, say to yourself,

"I am calming my brain with a smile."

Your Journal

Quietly reflect on your activities today. What did you discover about yourself? Write. Draw. Doodle.

Now it's time for the
WagiCheer!
See page 24

Get Feedback!

When we brainstormed, we learned how to walk in the shoes of a Brainstormer and compassionately create ideas by asking three questions:

1. "What if?"

2. "Why is this a good idea?"

3. "What would we **never** do?"

Today, we are going to get feedback from others to learn what they think about our ideas. Sharing your ideas is important because, when you put your heart into creating an idea, it can be hard for you to judge whether the idea is good, great, or just OK.

Getting comments from other people can help you think about your idea and make it better. Their thoughts and suggestions can also give you the confidence to keep going and make your idea a reality.

When you show your idea to your friends and family, it's easy for them to simply say that they like it. The best way to get more honest and helpful feedback is to ask specific questions to help others give the information you need.

So, Team One, you're up first! Describe your idea and show any pictures you've made. Talk about the challenge in your community and how your idea will solve the problem.

After presenting your idea, have team members take turns asking the following questions.

Feedback Questions:

1. Do you understand our idea? Is there anything you don't understand? If so, how can we make our idea clearer? Write down feedback.

2. What do you like most about our idea?

3. Do you think our idea will work? If not, what could we do to make it work? Would you help us create our idea?

4. If this idea was yours, how would you change it?

5. If the price of our product or service was $_____, would you buy it? If yes, great. If no, what's stopping you from buying?

After Team One gets feedback, have the other teams present their ideas, and take feedback notes.

So, How Did It Go?

Did you get positive comments?

Did some comments sound critical or negative?

Take them all in! Remember, the comments are about the ideas, not about YOU!

If the feedback makes you feel frustrated, you know what to do. **STOP** and Smile!

Most importantly, you are in charge. If your team disagrees with a comment, you don't have to use it. You can keep your idea just the way it is.

Review the Feedback:

As all inventors know, both positive and negative feedback can help your team improve your ideas. Try it and see!

Take fifteen minutes with your team to discuss the feedback and see how you can use the advice to improve your idea. Fill out the feedback sheet on the next page.

WagiInventor Tip:

Sometimes, feedback helps you realize that some of your ideas won't work.

If so, now's the time to let go of the ideas and create something new! In the idea world, letting go of an idea is called "**pivoting**."

Feedback Sheet

Use the feedback you got to help you think of ways to improve your idea. Write your new ideas below.

Feedback: _____

_____

Improvements: _____

_____

Feedback: _____

_____

Improvements: _____

_____

Feedback: _____

_____

Improvements: _____

_____

Feedback: _____

_____

Improvements: _____

_____

"Sniff Test"

When Wagi goes for a treat, he always gives a quick sniff with his snout. Why? He wants to make sure it is safe to eat. He does what we call the "Sniff Test."

It's based on the Golden Rule?

"Do unto others as you would have them do unto you."

The rule is a guideline for understanding what is right or wrong. Here's a "Sniff Test" Checklist to apply to your new idea so you can be sure you have done your best to make everything right.

If you answer "No" to any question, talk to your teammates and brainstorm ways to improve your idea so you can answer, "Yes!"

1. Do I believe in our idea?   Yes ❏ No ❏

2. Would I use it or buy it?   Yes ❏ No ❏

3. Is our idea fair to everyone?   Yes ❏ No ❏

4. Will our idea help solve the problem we found?   Yes ❏ No ❏

5. Is our idea safe for humans, animals and the environment?   Yes ❏ No ❏

6. Did everyone on my team get a chance to contribute to the idea?   Yes ❏ No ❏

7. Is everyone who contributed to our idea getting recognition?   Yes ❑ No ❑

8. Did we listen to feedback and make our idea better?   Yes ❑ No ❑

9. Would I want to explain everything about our idea to my friends?   Yes ❑ No ❑

10. Would I be proud to show our idea on the news and share it on social media?   Yes ❑ No ❑

Necessary Improvements:

Improvements: _____

_____

Improvements: _____

_____

Improvements: _____

_____

Improvements: _____

_____

Improvements: _____

_____

Your Journal

Quietly reflect on your activities today. What did you discover about yourself? Write. Draw. Doodle.

Now it's time for the
WagiCheer!
See page 24

You are now entering the

Ocean of Courage!

Your mission will be to:

☐ Build Your Prototypes

Now that we have ideas, it is time to experiment with possible solutions. Let's build prototypes and share them with others.

☐ Plan Your Pitch

What's the best way to present our ideas? A perfect pitch, of course! Let's learn how to tell a story that makes our ideas irresistible!

☐ Create a Music Video

Writing a song can help you tell your story.

☐ Present Your Pitch

It's show time — time to present our ideas to the panel of coaches, who will help us make our ideas a reality.

Courage

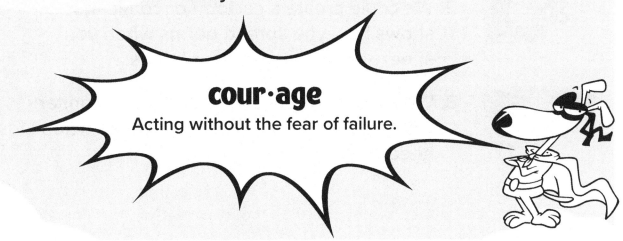

cour·age

Acting without the fear of failure.

Build Your Prototypes!

It takes courage to make your ideas visible for the world to see. Let's experiment with our ideas and build prototypes of our proposed solutions.

Some prototypes, such as sketches or storyboards show what your idea looks like. Others, like mock-ups or models, demonstrate how your idea works. Best of all, once you make a prototype, you can show it to others to get feedback and keep improving your idea.

Here are examples of prototypes designed to reduce spreading cold germs among school kids — a big uncovered need!!!

Prototype Examples:

What are prototypes like? Here are some examples. When kids tried to think of ways to help their friends stop spreading cold germs in school, they came up with these prototype ideas.

1. We could design a fun facemask for children to wear when they have a cold.

2. We could create a cartoon or comic that shows how you spread germs when you sneeze or don't wash your hands.

3. We could create a cool way to carry sanitary wipes, so it's easy to hand out wipes when kids need them.

4. We could teach kids to sing a song while washing their hands so they know when they have washed long enough to kill the germs.

A facemask, a comic, a wipe container, and a song — each of these prototypes is very different, yet all of them try to solve the same problem! Now it's time for each team to design and build a prototype to show off their ideas.

The Steps to Design a Prototype:

1. Draw a detailed sketch of your idea. Plan carefully. Include all of the parts that make it work.

2. When your sketch is finished, check out the materials you have in your WagiLab. What can you use to build each part? Make a list of the materials you will need.

3. Finally, make a list of the jobs your team members will need to do to build the prototype. Decide who will do each job. You can work together on jobs, too!

4. Gather the materials you are going to use. Keep them organized so you can find each one when you need it.

5. Build your prototype. If you are going to draw your final prototype, start drawing.

6. At any time, if you are not happy with your prototype, change it! If some of your pieces don't work, try different pieces, or different ways to make each part.

7. If your prototype doesn't work, you might have to change your idea or make a new prototype. **Don't give up!** It's all part of the invention process!

Presenting your Prototypes:

We started by getting feedback about our ideas. Now it's time to show each other our prototypes and get more feedback. Just like when you presented your ideas, try not to be disappointed if some feedback sounds critical or negative. Even these comments can help you make your idea better.

Team One, you're up first! Tell everyone about your prototype. Then, ask at least two of the following questions to get feedback from your friends:

1. Do you understand our idea? Is there anything you don't understand? If so, how can we make our idea clearer?

2. Do you think our idea will work? If not, what can we do to make it work?

3. What do you like most about our idea?

4. If this idea were yours, how would you change it?

Write down every suggestion and thank your WagiMates for their feedback. After Team One gets feedback, give each of the other teams a chance to present and take notes.

Review the Feedback:

Now take ten minutes to talk about the feedback and see if you can use it to improve your prototype and idea.

Feedback: _____

_____

Improvements: _____

_____

Feedback: _____

_____

Improvements: _____

_____

Feedback: _____

_____

Improvements: _____

_____

Feedback: _____

_____

Improvements: _____

A Cool Experiment

Question: Why does ice melt when you take it out of the freezer?

1. Ice Cube Warm-Up Exercise

Challenge: To find out how fast the heat of your body (~98.6 degrees) will melt an ice cube.

How long do you think it will take to melt the ice cube? _____

1. Team up with four kids and form a line.

2. The first kid in each line receives an ice cube.

3. Start the timer.

4. The first kid rubs the ice cube between their hands for as long as they can to see how quickly the ice cube can melt.

5. Once that kid's hand gets too cold, the ice cube is passed to the next kid in line.

6. The first team to melt the ice cube wins!

How long did it take to melt the ice cube? _____

If you could rerun the exercise, does your team have ideas on how to melt the ice cube faster?

1.

2.

3.

Rerun the exercise with a new ice cube.

How long did it take to melt the ice cube? _____

2. Ice Cube Melt-Off!!! Experiment

If we want to keep ice from melting, we need to insulate it. We need to keep warm gases, solids, and liquids from touching it.

Challenge: To find materials that are good insulators and will keep an ice cube from melting.

Activity: Which ice cube will melt first, one on a metal pan or one on a plastic board?

Hypothesis: Which surface will allow the ice cube to melt first?

◻ Metal Pan ◻ Plastic Board

1. Touch the metal and plastic surfaces, does one surface feel different than the other?

2. Place one ice cube on a plastic board and another on a metal pan.

3. Start the timer. Watch the progress of the ice cube melting and record the times.

Which surface allowed the ice cube to melt first?

◻ Metal Pan ◻ Plastic Board

Why?

3. Vaccine Transport Design Experiment

Imagine that you are a healthcare provider who needs to transport a vaccine from your office, which has a refrigeration unit for vaccines, to a patient who is unable to come into your office to be vaccinated.

The vaccine will be out of the refrigerator for sixty minutes while you transport it to the patient.

Challenge: You need to design an insulated container that you can carry, that will hold the vaccine and keep it cool.

For this experiment, you will use an ice cube to simulate the vaccine. You want to keep it from melting! You will design a container with insulation materials to act as the transport unit.

Create as many insulated containers as you would like with the insulation materials.

Design Process:

1. Decide what materials, or combinations of materials, you want to use to insulate your ice cube.

2. Draw your vaccine transport container design.

3. Get feedback from others on your design.

4. Redesign your transport container, incorporating feedback.

5. Build at least one vaccine transport container. If time allows, build more than one.

6. Set your insulated containers in an area away from sunlight or direct heat source.

Testing the Transport Container:

1. Obtain an ice cube. Place it on a scale to determine its mass in grams. Record this in your data table.

2. Place the ice cube into your vaccine transport container and start the timer.

3. After ten minutes, take the mass of your ice cube as quickly as possible and return it to the vaccine transport container. Record the weight in the data table.

4. Continue to record the mass of the ice cube every ten minutes for sixty minutes.

5. Graph the results.

6. Compare your results to determine which container design worked best insulating the ice cube from melting.

Data Collection and Analysis:

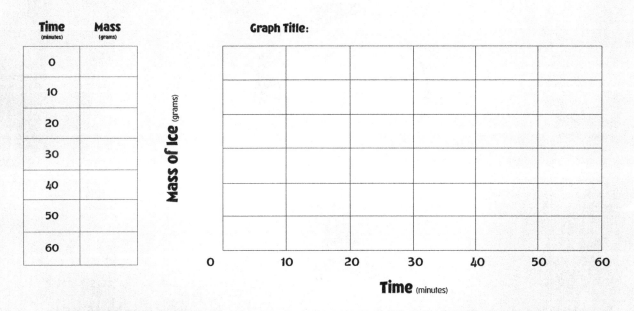

Time (minutes)	Mass (grams)
0	
10	
20	
30	
40	
50	
60	

Graph Title:

Mass of Ice (grams) vs. Time (minutes)

1. What happened to the mass of the ice cube over time?

2. How does your ice cube compare to your friends'?

3. What are the characteristics of the containers that worked the best to keep the vaccine cold?

Mindful Moment

Ocean Breath

You've had so many ideas swirling around in your brain that it can be hard to slow down your mind.

You can use a special kind of breath to let your brain know that it's time to calm down. It's called the ocean breath.

Let's try it. Take a slow, deep breath in and let your belly get big. When you breathe out, make an "**HAAAA**" sound with your breath, like you're trying to fog up a mirror.

When you breathe this way, you make a sound like the ocean or Darth Vader! After you've taken three or four "ocean" breaths, your body will feel calmer, and your brain will slow down so you can focus on one idea at a time.

Your Journal

Quietly reflect on your activities today. What did you discover about yourself? Write. Draw. Doodle.

Now it's time for the
WagiCheer!
See page 24

Plan Your Pitch!

What's the best way to present your ideas to your classmates, parents, teachers, and your community? A pitch, of course!

A pitch is a story to get people excited about your idea. It tells why your solution is needed and makes people want to support your idea.

Let's learn how to tell a story that makes your ideas shine by creating turning our pitch into a movie script, a highway billboard and then a music video.

Let's Create a Movie Script

Have you seen the movie "Toy Story?" Stories like this often start out with these three words: "Once upon a time..."

In giving pitches, they usually start out with:

- "Every day ..."
- "Every time..."
- "I'm going to tell you about a big challenge ..."

Work with your teammates to write the introduction to your pitch for your challenge. Write about who has the challenge in a way that makes us really care about them.

The more exciting your pitch is, the more people will get into it — just like an exciting movie.

1. Start the Story: Grab Everyone's Attention!

Tell about the challenge and where it happens. Start with the words "Every day ..." or, if the challenge only happens sometimes, you might use the words "Every time ..." Be dramatic!

2. Add Plot Details: Make Everyone Care!

Tell more about how the challenge affects people. Expand on Step One by showing how the challenge keeps happening and no one has fixed it yet.

3. Be the Hero: Share Your Idea!

Here comes the best part of your story — the big idea! Tell everyone your solution to the problem, how you thought of it, and why it's such a great idea! You might start with the words "Until one day..." or "We know what to do!"

4. Save the Day: Tell How It Works!

Now tell how your idea solves the challenge.

5. Have a Happy Ending: End with a Bang!

Tell how everyone will live happily ever after!

Finally, tell how people can help and what life will be like after the challenge is solved.

Computer Animation!

Consider adding some computer animation to your pitch! It's easy to get started.

1. Go to https://scratch.mit.edu and click "Start Creating."

2. Watch the tutorial video to learn the basics, then click the green arrow to continue learning.

3. You can try out any new skills you have learned on the Scratch website.

4. At any time, you can click "Tutorials" on the top menu to help you learn more.

5. Try these tutorials to help you get started: Code a Cartoon and Create a Story.

6. If you want to create a music video, try the Record a Sound and Make Music tutorials.

Let's Create an Idea Pitch Billboard!

Imagine you are riding in a car and see a billboard next to the road or giant poster on a building.

Can you read the message in thirty seconds and know what it is saying? You bet! That's because billboards have big, bold pictures and very few words. They are designed to capture your attention in a "flash" before you pass.

Billboards have four main parts: the slogan, the call to action, the captivating picture, and the contact information.

Slogan: "A Shelter Pet Wants to Meet You."

Call to Action: Adopt logo with pawprint inside of hand

Picture: an adorable cat

Contact Information: TheShelterPetProject.org

Now, it's time to create a billboard sign that tells the world about your idea.

Follow these five guidelines.

1. Use Ten Words or Less!

A slogan is a "catchy," saying that tells about your idea. The shorter, the better. Think about the famous slogans that you see every day.

JUST DO IT.

i'm lovin' it™

Come up with a list of at least five slogans you think will give you ideas to help sell your pitch.

1.

2.

3.

4.

5.

Then, take fifteen minutes to come up with two slogans for your idea. Make them "catchy" so people will remember them.

_____

_____

2. Create a Call to Action!

What is one-way people can make your idea happen?

_____

_____

3. Use a Great Picture to Show Off Your Idea!

Make a drawing, cut out pictures, or use a photograph.

4. Add Contact Information:

Add your website address and a phone number in large letters.

_____

_____

5. Share Your Billboards with Other Teams:

1. Did they understand your slogan?

2. Did they like your picture?

3. Did it grab their attention?

4. Did it make them want to act?

5. What feedback do they have to improve your billboard?

Feedback: _____

_____

Improvements: _____

_____

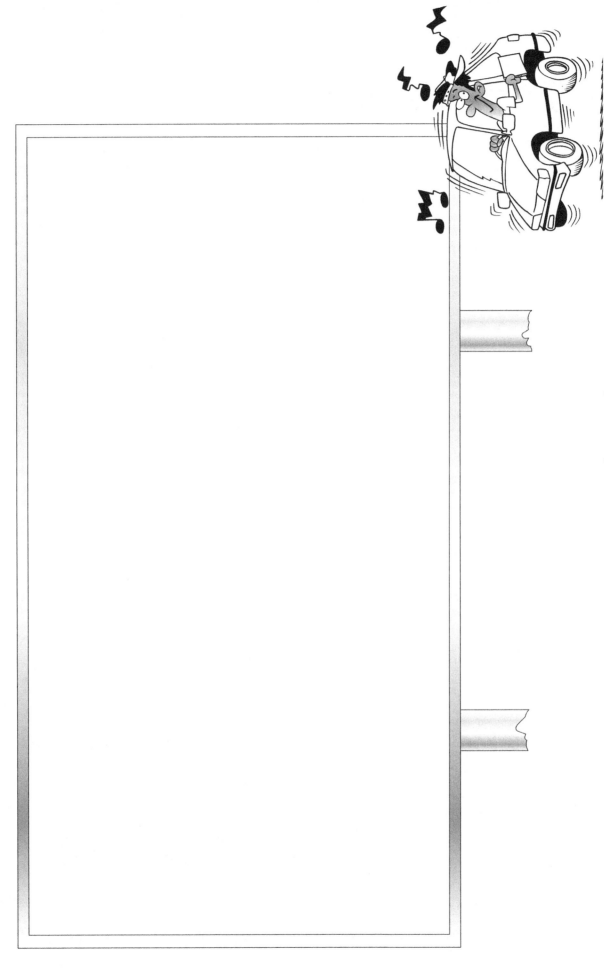

Create Your Idea Pitch Billboard

Your Journal

Quietly reflect on your activities today. What did you discover about yourself? Write. Draw. Doodle.

Now it's time for the
WagiCheer!
See page 24

Let's Create a Music Video!

Where Words Paired with Music Can Change the World!

Why Do We Write Songs?

As one musician recently said, "When talking just isn't enough!" What makes a song different from merely talking? The music, of course!

When you put words to music, it's easier for other people to connect with them! They can feel the beat in their bodies. They can hear your emotions when the notes and rhythms change.

Writing a song can be one of the best ways to tell a story about how you feel. Sometimes, singing makes it easier to share sad feelings. Other times, a song can be an amazing way to celebrate happy feelings.

Writing a song can also help you tell a story about something important to you. That's just what you're going to do at WagiLabs!

GOALS:

1. Write a song about your identified community challenge.

2. Tell others about the challenge, and share your ideas for hopeful solutions.

3. Make listeners excited, so they want to get involved.

The Lyrics Tell the Story

The words of a song are called lyrics. There are two big rules to follow when you write the lyrics of any song.

1. Good lyrics paint a picture for the listeners, so that they can see the people, places, and problems in the story.

2. Great lyrics also help listeners put themselves in your shoes and feel your emotions! Every songwriter's goal is to write lyrics that bring the story to life.

The Music Makes a Song More Memorable

While the words of a song tell the story, the music can help set the mood and draw in listeners. Most important, the music helps others remember the story because they can sing along.

Think of your favorite songs. Can you hum the melody for each one? Do the words and music stick in your head? Good music can make a song unforgettable!

Listen Up!

A group of WagiKids in Ghana wrote a song called "Everyday Wash" about healthy hand washing. The first part is sung in English, and the second is sung in Twi, one of the languages spoken in Ghana. Watch the kids from Ghana Cocoa 360 sing:

https://tinyurl.com/everydaywash

What Did You Hear?

1. Can you hear the story in the lyrics?

2. Can you see the story in the video?

3. Can you feel the beat?

4. How does the music make you feel?

Look at Lyrics

1. Circle your favorite lyrics. What message do they tell?

2. Circle words that repeat. What makes it memorable?

3. Circle words that rhyme.

Bath, bath, bath,

Everyday bath!

Wash, wash, wash,

Everyday wash!

Bath everyday,

Wash twice a day!

Washroom, wash your hands,

After playtime ends!

Shake hands with friends,

Stay happy, healthy, and STRONG!

Bath, bath, bath,

Everyday bath!

Wash, wash, wash,

Everyday wash!

Bath everyday,

Wash twice a day!

Washroom, wash your hands,

After playtime ends!

Shake hands with friends,

Stay happy, healthy, and strong!

Bath, bath, bath,

Everyday bath!

Look at Lyrics (in Twi and Compare to English)

1. Circle your favorite lyrics.

2. Circle words that repeat. Do the same words repeat?

3. Circle words that rhyme. Do the same words rhyme?

Enti dware, dware, dware,
Dware mmienu!
Hohoro, hohoro, hohoro,
Hohoro wɔ nsa!
Sɛ wu gyae wɔ ne ba,
Hohoro wɔ nsa!
Sɛ wɔ kɔ di agorɔ ba,
Hohoro wɔ nsa!
Ɛnona ɛbɛ ma wo,
Apomu din ahon din debiya!
Enti dware, dware, dware,
Dware mmienu!
Hohoro, hohoro, hohoro,
Hohoro wɔ nsa!
Sɛ wu gyae wɔ ne ba,
Hohoro wɔ nsa!
Sɛ wɔ kɔ di agorɔ ba,
Hohoro wɔ nsa!
Ɛnona ɛbɛ ma wo,
Apomu din ahon din debiya!
Enti dware, dware, dware,
Dware mmienu!

Think Like a Detective...

What's the story in the song? Remember, one of the two rules of writing a song is that it tells a story.

What story do you think the kids are trying to tell?

Why is it important to wash every day?

How do you think the "Everyday Wash" song will help people in the kids' community? What will they do differently?

How do you think the kids from Ghana will feel if their song helps people in their community stay healthy?

Do you think this song can help kids and adults in communities outside of Ghana?

The Four Parts of a Song

Songs including "Everyday Wash" are made up of four parts: verses, a chorus, a bridge, and a coda.

As a songwriter, you can choose some or all of these parts to tell your story.

VERSES:

The verses of a song usually describe the situation or challenge and tell the details: "what, why, who, when, and where" of your story.

CHORUS:

The chorus tells the main message of your story in such a catchy way so people can't help singing along.

BRIDGE:

The bridge is usually halfway through the song and has the highest and most intense singing in it. It adds more meaning to your song before bringing the listener back to the chorus.

CODA/RAP:

The word "coda" means tail or ending. The coda is a short, extra ending for a song. It's a way to make sure listeners remember your message!

Now it's time to write your song!

WagiMusic Songsheet

Student Name: _____ Team: _____

Song Title: _____

Your Community Challenge:

_____
_____
_____
_____
_____

Key Words that Describe the Challenge:

_____
_____
_____
_____
_____
_____
_____

Key Words that Describe Your Solution:

_____
_____
_____
_____
_____
_____
_____

Draw It!

Draw a picture of the challenge and your solution on this page. Use the picture to help you answer the five "W" questions on the next page.

Answer the Five "W" Questions:

Use the picture you drew on the previous page to help you answer these questions.

WHAT is our goal? **WHAT** do people need?

_____

_____

_____

_____

_____

_____

WHY do we want to achieve the goal or result described in the first question?

_____

_____

_____

_____

_____

_____

WHO has the need or is facing the challenge?

_____

_____

_____

_____

_____

_____

WHEN does the challenge occur?

WHERE does the challenge occur?

Now Focus on Your Feelings!

How do you want listeners to feel when they hear your song?
List their emotions?

Write Your Lyrics:

If you chose a song first, play the music and write your words to match the rhythm and beat.

Verse 1:

Chorus 1:

Verse 2 (Optional):

_____

_____

_____

_____

_____

_____

_____

_____

_____

_____

_____

_____

Bridge (Optional):

_____

_____

_____

_____

_____

_____

_____

_____

_____

_____

_____

_____

Coda (Optional):

Now Come Up with a Title:

Brainstorm five titles for your song. Is there a word or phrase that tells the whole message? Is there a line you really like, or one that repeats a lot? Write the potential song titles below.

Compose Your Music:

1. If you wrote your song lyrics first, write your music now.

2. Start singing your lyrics and make up the melody as you go along.

3. Sing one line at a time or sing a whole section.

4. Tap the rhythm of the lyrics on a drum or table.

5. Then, begin singing notes that you think match.

6. If you have a keyboard, piano, or other instrument, use it to experiment with different melodies.

7. Use the online Chrome Music Labs: Song Maker tool for inspiration. Try this link to explore Song Maker!

   https://bit.ly/2oJglWV

8. Be sure to use an audio recorder to record each melody you compose! Then you won't forget your tunes, and you can listen and sing along to see which one you like best.

Edit Your Music:

1. Come up with different melodies. Combine them. Keep parts you like and throw others out.

2. Keep experimenting until you have written music for each part of the song. Play it back. Sing along.

3. When you're done, CELEBRATE!!! Your song will raise awareness of your community challenge.

Sing Your Music:

1. Now open both your mouths AND your hearts and SING!

2. Record your singing so you can play it back.

3. Listen closely. Is everyone singing the right words and notes?

4. Does the rhythm feel right?

5. Practice your song until you know it and love it! Then, share it! Sing loudly and proudly for everyone you know.

WagiMusic Video

When you tell your story using pictures and songs, you make it easier for people to see the community challenge and your solution. A music video lets you sing about your ideas and show them to the world!

Think Visually:

Imagine your challenge coming to life!

1. What are people doing in the first scene?

2. Where are they?

3. Are they holding things or using props?

4. How does the action change in the next scene?

5. How do the actors solve the challenge?

6. Write your ideas in the chart on the next page.

Visual Worksheet

SCENE LOCATION	ACTORS	ACTIONS	PROPS

Make a Storyboard:

Draw pictures to show what happens in each scene of your music video (draw simple figures or cut out people and objects). Use your song lyrics to help you think of ideas.

Write the matching song lyrics under each picture, and add video tips to help the videographer know how to shoot the scene.

Finally, line up the pictures in order, so they show your whole movie from the first scene to the last.

You can use the storyboard form on the next page.

Shoot Your Video:

Use your storyboard to help you decide what to shoot. Be sure to record all of the scenes that you drew on your sticky notes.

Production Tips

1. Record the audio many times in different ways; listen to and sing your song and listen to it until you know the words and rhythms by heart.

2. Record each scene multiple times from different angles and in different ways; you might even want to record the same action in different places.

3. Shoot more video than you think you need; you can always discard the clips you don't use.

4. When you are done shooting your video, review your clips together, and save your favorites in a "BEST VIDEOS" folder. Be sure a few people review the clips to be sure you didn't overlook some great shots!

WagiStoryBoard

Title:

Date:

Description:

Description:

Description:

Action:
Dialog:
F/X:

Description:

Description:

Description:

Action:
Dialog:
F/X:

Action:

Action:

Action:

135

Edit Your Video:

You'll need to choose which editing app you'll use to put your video together.

Once you have the videos selected and have added your song to the editing application, it's time to begin editing.

Production Tips

As edit, line up each video clip with the audio that matches so it feels like the actors are singing the song.

Match the rhythm of the action to the rhythm of your music; match the images in the video with the emotions of your song.

Combine the video clips. You don't have to use a whole clip. Choose pieces of the best videos and stitch them together. Some will be short, and some will be longer.

Play your video after you make a change whether it's finish a section, add a clip, so on. Feel free to shorten clips, and move them around until the flow seems perfect!

Play It and Share It!

When you finish your music video — CELEBRATE!!!

Play it and watch it as many times as you like. Congratulate each other for all your hard work.

Then share it with everyone you know — especially people who can learn from it.

Your Journal

Quietly reflect on your activities today. What did you discover about yourself? Write. Draw. Doodle.

Now it's time for the
WagiCheer!
See page 24

Present Your Pitch!

It's GuppyTank Day!

Today, we are celebrating the hard work of our WagiLabs teams. You have used your detective skills to uncover needs in our community and your brainstorming skills to come up with ideas to help solve those needs.

Now it's time for you to present your ideas to the WagiLabs coaches and mentors who have helped you on your missions. Perhaps, people from the community will be invited, too.

Go, Go, Show, Show!

Here's how the GuppyTank works. Each team gets **three minutes** to pitch their idea and **five minutes** to get feedback.

Hints for the Teams:

1. Follow storyboarding outline and act out your pitch.

2. Show your prototype and use your billboard and (slogan or song) so everyone remembers your idea.

3. Be energetic, and don't read the words — tell the story.

4. Cheer for each other!

5. When the coaches are answering your questions, be sure that one of your team members takes notes.

Now it's time to practice a **Mindful Moment** to relax and center your thoughts before your presentation.

Mindful Moment

Float on the Ocean

1. Close your eyes and Imagine floating on the ocean.

2. Make a smile with each breath and notice how your face changes.

3. Do your cheeks move up? Do your lips open?

4. Does your jaw relax? Keep breathing and smiling.

5. Relax and imagine you are floating for sixty seconds.

6. Now take your smile with you for the rest of the day.

After Your Pitch:

After you do your pitch, ask some of the following questions to get feedback from your coaches and others in the audience:

1. Did you understand our idea? Is there anything you didn't understand? If so, how can we make our idea clearer?

2. What things do you like the most about our idea?

3. If this was your idea, how would you change it?

4. Do you think we can make this idea happen?

5. If not, what ideas do you have to help us make it happen?

6. How did our idea make you feel?

Responses to Feedback Questions:

1. How can we make our idea clearer?

2. What things do you like most about our idea?

3. If this was your idea, how would you change it?

4. Do you think we can make this idea happen?
   Why or why not?

5. If not, what can we do to make it happen?

6. How did our idea make you feel?

How Do You Feel About Your GuppyTank Pitch?

Were you nervous? Excited? What was the best part?

1.

2.

3.

4.

What Did You Learn?

1.

2.

3.

4.

What Changes Will You Make?

How will you change your pitch the next time you present?

1.

2.

3.

4.

What is Your Score?

Now that all of the WagiTeams have made their pitches, the GuppyTank coaches will get together to discuss each team's idea. Here's a copy of the Idea ScoreCard that shows how the coaches will be evaluating your ideas.

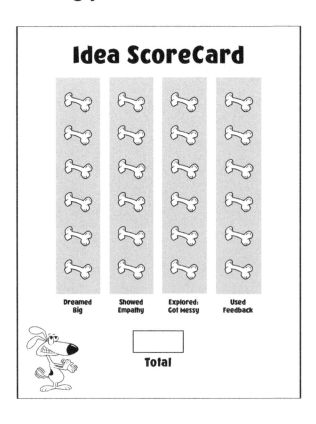

Your Journal

Quietly reflect on your activities today. What did you discover about yourself? Write. Draw. Doodle.

Now it's time for the
WagiCheer!
See page 24

Make it Happen!

Great ideas are only great when we make them happen. Today, we're going to talk about how to get the help we need to turn our ideas into real products and services!

Mentors and You:

Anytime you start something new, you have a lot to learn. This is especially true when you are working on a new idea or starting a new business or service.

Working with the right advisors or mentors can help you save time, improve your idea, and avoid making mistakes.

Together, take time to brainstorm mentors who might help each team develop their product or service.

Possibilities include:

1. Relative/friend

2. Community member

3. Teacher

4. Business person

5. Someone who provides or sells a similar product/service

6. Expert who knows how to make the product/service

Come up with a list of three possible mentors for each team.

1. _____

2. _____

3. _____

Now, with your team, pick one mentor from your list to write to for help and guidance.

Make It Write:

Now that you've chosen a mentor you want to contact, what should you write? What do you want to tell your potential adviser about your idea?

Brainstorm what you might want to say in your letter. Be sure to explain what your idea is and how people will use it. Also include a drawing or photo of the prototype.

1.

2.

3.

OK, let's write our mentor letters. Come up with your own letter, or use the letter on the next page as a guide.

Mentor Letter Example

_____
(DATE)

Hi Mr./Ms./Dr. _____,

My name is _____, and I am _____ years old.

I am working with my WagiLabs team to come up with ideas that help make life better for people in our neighborhood — and, we hope, around the world.

We are trying to solve the problem of:

My team is very interested in this problem because:

To solve the problem, we came up with this idea:

We have attached a picture (or pictures) that shows our _____. (IDEA)

We are really excited to move forward with our idea, but we need help learning more about what to do. We think you would be a good person to talk to because:

We hope that you will be interested in talking to us and helping us make our idea better.

Best wishes,

P.S. To learn more about WagiLabs, go to: www.wagilabs.org and @ wagilabs on Instagram and Twitter.

Step-by-Step Checklist

What do you have to do to turn your idea into a real product, project or service? Check the box next to each step you have to do to make your product happen.

Get More Feedback by:

☐ Meeting with mentors

☐ Showing idea/prototype to children and/or adults

☐ Talking to people who will help manufacture our product

☐ Talking to people who will help distribute our product

Research other Products/Services by:

☐ Looking in Stores

☐ Searching on the internet

Test and Improve Our Prototype by:

☐ Making a list of materials we need to make our product

☐ Scheduling time to work on the prototype or service

☐ Testing samples of real products and service

Create Artwork or Pictures by:

☐ Searching for and for free Clip art and images on Google

☐ Downloading free music

Raise Money for Manufacturing/Marketing by:

- [ ] Having a toy or bake sale
- [ ] Offering services such as dog walking and babysitting
- [ ] Conducting a crowdfunding campaign

Create a Brand by:

- [ ] Coming up with a name for our product or service
- [ ] Designing a logo
- [ ] Writing a slogan
- [ ] Writing a mission statement that explains our goal

Create Instructions for Our Product by:

- [ ] Writing instructions telling how to use our Product
- [ ] Writing descriptions to use on packaging
- [ ] Writing descriptions for our website

Market Our Product by:

- [ ] Finding out how similar products/services are marketed
- [ ] Creating a website
- [ ] Creating a brochure or poster
- [ ] Creating a video
- [ ] Turning your storyboard into a social media campaign
- [ ] Creating an ad for a local flier, newspaper or radio

Timeline for Your Idea!

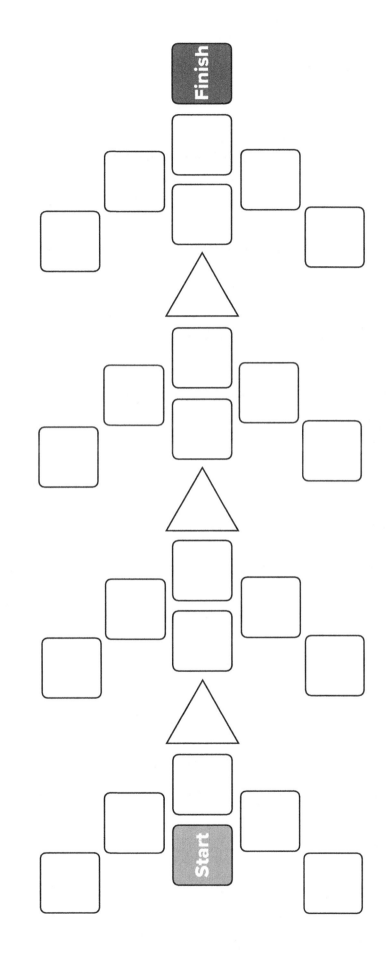

You'll have to do many steps to make your ideas happen. A timeline can help you plan which steps to do first and which come later.

Fill in the squares with the steps you need to do. Start with the most important steps first!

149

Build Trust!

As a kidpreneur, you want your customers to think of you as a trustworthy supplier, even if you are giving your product/service away for free.

So here's another checklist, like the earlier "Sniff Test" on page 94, to help you think about your new idea.

If you answer **"NO"** to any question, talk to your teammates and brainstorm ways to improve your idea.

1. Be Transparent (that means, be open and honest)

Have you revealed to your customer:

- All materials used in product/service? Yes ❏ No ❏

- Their total cost for the product/service? Yes ❏ No ❏

- Your return or refund policy? Yes ❏ No ❏

- How to contact you if any questions? Yes ❏ No ❏

- Will you give a receipt after purchase? Yes ❏ No ❏

2. Advertise Honestly (always tell the truth)

Are you giving any false impressions regarding:

- Popularity of your product/service? Yes ❑ No ❑
- Recommendations for product/service? Yes ❑ No ❑
- Benefits of product/service? Yes ❑ No ❑
- Quality of product/service? Yes ❑ No ❑

3. Honor Promises (what you've said about your product)

Will you be responsive to customers about:

- Correcting any mistakes? Yes ❑ No ❑
- Resolving any complaints? Yes ❑ No ❑
- Handling returns? Yes ❑ No ❑
- Giving back refunds? Yes ❑ No ❑

4. Remember...

Your Product/Service is your promise of
quality and reliability.

Mindful Moment

Shake It Out!

1. Stand up straight. Breathe in and hold your breath.

2. Breathe out and shake out your arms and hands. Shake them high and then shake them low.

3. Breathe in and hold your breath.

4. Breathe out and shake out your legs and your feet.

5. Breathe in and hold your breath.

6. Breathe out and shake your whole body until it feels loose.

7. Now take three long, slow breaths, and return to your wonderful day.

Your Journal

Quietly reflect on your activities today. What did you discover about yourself? Write. Draw. Doodle.

Now it's time for the
WagiCheer!
See page 24

Play It Forward!

In our very last session, you'll think about your WagiLab experiences and plan a talk to tell other kids about them.

Sharing what you have learned in WagiLabs is called "Playing It Forward." It's one way to spread the word about doing good – so more kids help more people!

Share the WagiWays:

You've grown since our first day in the WagiLab, and so have your ideas! These eight WagiWays have guided us as we worked together.

Create WagiWays Cards:

Make copies of the WagiWays cards starting on page 156. Then cut each page in half (on the dotted line), and fold the cards so the name is on one side and the description is on the other.

Play with the WagiWays:

Spread out the WagiWay cards face down and choose a card. Take time to read the description on the back of your card.

Today, you're going to help other kids learn what it's like to be a Kidpreneur by talking about the WagiWay on the card you picked.

- Start by telling what you were like or how you looked at things before coming to the WagiLabs.

- Then tell how using the WagiWay helped you learn or change, what you learned, and why you want other kids to know about it.

Before:

1.

2.

3.

After:

1.

2.

3.

By sharing your WagiLabs thoughts and experiences, and telling how you have grown, you can help other kids "walk in **YOUR** shoes," and see how they might grow, too.

Dream Big!

Do Good!

Dream Big!

To live life to the fullest, dream big. At WagiLabs, we try to think of ideas that are innovative and can help many people. Dreaming big helps us do things that can change the world. What did you learn at WagiLabs to help you dream big?

Do Good!

At WagiLabs, doing good means coming up with ideas to help people and make the world a better place. We focus on giving rather than receiving, and acting on our ideas instead of just thinking about them. What did you learn at WagiLabs to help you do good?

Walk in Others' Shoes!

Walk in Others' Shoes!

At WagiLabs, other people inspire us to come up with ideas. When we put ourselves in other people's shoes, we see what they see or feel what they feel. Understanding others in this way is called having "empathy." What did you learn at WagiLabs to help you walk in others' shoes?

Get Messy!

Get Messy!

At WagiLabs, getting messy means experimenting with ideas, models, and prototypes to come up with the best solution for a problem. Getting messy also includes getting feedback about our ideas and prototypes so we can improve them, and sometimes, letting go of ideas that don't work. What did you learn at WagiLabs to help you build a prototype and get messy?

Say YES, and...

Say "YES, and..."
WagiLabs is all about being positive. "YES, and..." means "I accept your idea... AND I'm ready for more!" Being open to ideas helps us learn from each other and come up with new and better ideas together. How did saying "YES, and..." help you work on ideas at WagiLabs?

Keep Going!

Keep Going!
At WagiLabs, we talked about how many steps it takes to make our ideas happen. Remembering to keep going means 'not giving up' even if an idea or prototype doesn't work at first, or if you have to make changes or work hard to make your idea happen. What did you learn at WagiLabs to help you keep going?

Keep Going and Going:

Wagi here! It's hard to believe we've come so far! Think about your WagiLabs experiences.

1. Was it always easy to try new things?

2. Were there times when you or your team had trouble doing something?

3. Did you give up, or did you stick with it until you made it happen?

I'd say that you have both "persistence" and "resilience."

Persistence means you keep trying to reach your goal even when you face obstacles.

Resilience means you bounce back and try different solutions when your first try doesn't work. When you put persistence and resilience together, you get "grit."

Persistence + Resilience = Grit

And, for sure, you're going to need more grit to keep working on your idea before it becomes real.

Let's brainstorm how having "grit" will help us make our ideas happen.

Your Steps to Grit:

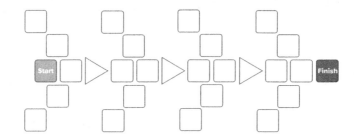

Look at the steps you filled into the "Timeline for Your Idea."

Choose the steps that might require persistence. Make a list of these tasks, and fill in your ideas about how having "grit" will help you do each task.

Steps	**Grit**
_____	_____
_____	_____
_____	_____
_____	_____
_____	_____
_____	_____
_____	_____
_____	_____

Wrap up:

Today we talked about "Playing It Forward" by teaching kids about the Wagi Ways and our mission to help others. We also talked about how having grit will help you move toward your goal of making your ideas happen.

Now, we have something for each one of you — it's the official WagiLabs Graduation Certificate of Kidpreneurship! There's a copy of the certificate on page 171.

Congratulations, WagiMates, you're on your way to changing the world!

WagiCelebration!!!

Remember the first day we came together? Most of you barely knew each other. Now, you're all part of the WagiLabs team — we've even walked in each other's shoes!

Thank you for coming to WagiLabs and sharing your ideas. Thank you for saying "Yes, **AND** ..." to other kids' ideas.

Together, we discovered our passions, uncovered social needs, defined a challenge, came up with ideas, and are on our way to making them happen.

Take a minute to thank your teammates for working with you and giving so much of themselves.

Keep Sharing and Sharing:

To help you share the WagiWays around the world, we hope you create a "Flat Wagi." It's easy!

When you're done, send out your Flat Wagi to kids you know in other neighborhoods, other states, and other countries. You can send your custom-made Wagi through the mail or email. Then keep track of and write about Flat Wagi's journey.

Steps for Creating a Flat Wagi:

1. Trace Wagi on the next page, draw your own picture of Wagi, or photograph Wagi.

2. Paste your picture on cardboard, and then cut it out in the shape of Wagi's body.

3. Be creative with coloring and accessorizing. Wagi loves to dress up and sometimes wear disguises!

4. Turn Wagi over and write your name, return address, and email on the back side.

5. Each time you send Flat Wagi to a friend, be sure to include a short letter describing your WagiLabs experiences and the challenges you are trying to solve. Maybe Flat Wagi's new friends will have ideas to help you and your team.

6. Ask your friends or others who get your Flat Wagi to take a picture that shows the moment when Wagi arrives, and write a description that tells who they are.

7. Share your photos with the hashtag #wagilabs for a chance to be featured on @wagilabs' Instagram page.

Creating Pen Pals:

To help you share the WagiWays around the world, we also hope you create Pen Pals. Just follow the steps below.

When you're done, send out your postcards through the mail to kids at WagiLabs in other neighborhoods, other states, and other countries.

Steps for Creating a Pen Pal:

1. Print the postcard design on the next page onto cover stock weight paper.

2. You can also design your postcard and use Wagi's design as inspiration. You postcard needs to be 4.25 inches by 6.0 inches in size. That's 10.8 cm by 15.24 cm.

3. You need to keep the front side white so that the post office can quickly read the address.

4. Write your name and return address in the upper left-hand section of the front side of the card.

5. Write your pen pal's name and address on the right side of the card below the postage area.

6. On the back, that's where there is space to tell your pen pal something about yourself and your challenge. Maybe your pen pal will have ideas to help you and your team?

7. The postcard can only be mailed once, so display the received cards on your wall.

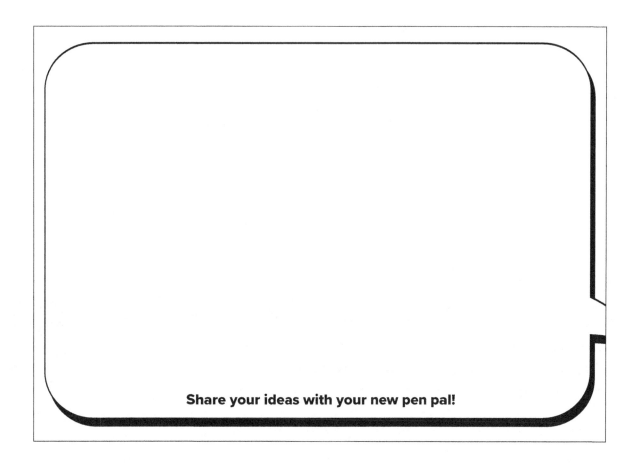

From:

_____

_____

_____

POSTAGE
REQUIRED

Dream
Big

Do Good

Keep Going

Yes, AND...

Play It
Forward

Get
Messy

Walk-in
Others' Shoes

Create a
Safe Space

To:

_____

_____

_____

_____

WagiLabs PostCard
wagilabs.org

Share your ideas with your new pen pal!

"Nine Dots" Final Exam

Can you connect these nine dots by drawing four straight lines? Once you start drawing the first line, you cannot lift your pencil or pen off the paper. You can draw across another line, but you can not retrace the same line.

Once you discover the solution, ask yourself: What did I learn by doing this exercise that will help me to solve challenges?

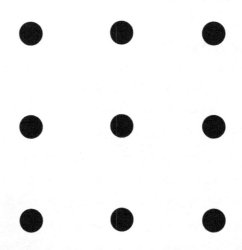

Here's a Hint:
You can draw lines that go past the dots to solve the puzzle.

Warning:
This exercise can get a little frustrating. If you need a break, you know what to do to calm yourself down!

Puzzle answer is on the bottom of page 169. Please don't peek.

Your Journal

Quietly reflect on your activities today. What did you discover about yourself? Write. Draw. Doodle.

Now it's time for the
WagiCheer!
See page 24

WagiPledge

We want to be best friends and to honor our loyalty we pledge the following:

FREE

WagiLabs will provide all teaching materials for free. Teachers will provide all WagiLabs sessions for free.

SHARE

WagiLabs will provide a teaching curriculum that all are welcome to customize to create the best learning experience for kids. Teachers will share their customized training sessions with other WagiLabs teachers to help them learn from shared experiences.

CREDIT

WagiLabs will provide our copyrighted materials. Teachers will highlight the WagiLabs logo in their teaching experience and social media posts.

FUNDING

WagiLabs is helping to fund some startup WagiLabs programs. Teachers will need to submit the Wagi Intake Form on page 172 along with a one-page proposal describing their funding needs. All funding recipients will need to sign and submit the necessary IRS tax forms that we send you. All WagiLabs funding can only be spent on WagiLabs activities and approved essential supplies.

_____   _____

WagiLabs Teacher/Facilitator   Date

_____   _____

WagiLabs Executive Director   Date

Resources

Here are additional materials to help you run a successful WagiLabs:

Printable Materials:

Wagi Pledge

Idea ScoreCard

Graduation Certificate

WagiLabs Intake Form

Pre-Launch Teachers Guide

Our WagiTeam:

Chic Thompson

Sandy Damashek

Lexi Hutchins

Julia Linn

Jennifer McKendree

Emmanuel Abebrese

Mary Porter Green

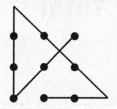

Idea ScoreCard

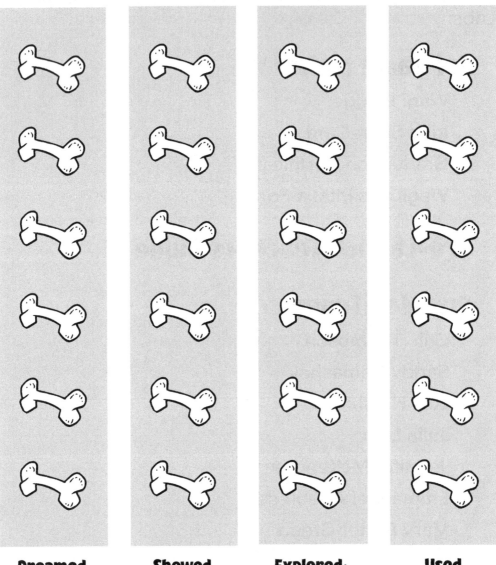

| Dreamed Big | Showed Empathy | Explored: Got Messy | Used Feedback |

Total

WagiLabs
IDEAS FOR GOOD!

Certificate of Kidpreneurship

Proudly presented to:

_____
Signed

_____
Date

Together, we discovered our passions, uncovered social needs, came up with ideas, and are on our way to making them happen. We changed the world!

WagiLabs Intake Form

"Help Us Customize Your WagiLabs Experience"

Contact Name: _____ Phone: _____

Organization: _____

Website: _____ email: _____

Street Address: _____ City: _____

State/Province: _____ Country: _____ State/Province: _____

Your Expected Outcomes from WagiLabs: (check as many as you like)

☐ Fun and Play

☐ Team Skills

☐ Uncover Social Needs

☐ Walk in Others' Shoes: Empathy

☐ Brainstorm Skills

☐ Critical Thinking Skills

☐ Generate Socially Responsive Ideas

☐ Build Idea Prototypes

☐ Tie into MakerSpace

☐ Tie into STEM

☐ Pitch Ideas

☐ Communication Skills

☐ Healthy Competition

☐ Learn How to Make Ideas Happen

☐ Time Management Skills

☐ Find Funding and Mentors for Ideas

☐ Global Exchange of Ideas with other Kids

☐ Learn to "Pivot" when Ideas Don't Work

☐ "Play it Forward" to other Kids

☐ Other: _____

Demographics of Your Kids:

1. Age Range: _____

2. Background: _____

3. Reading Level: _____

4. Primary Language: _____

5. Secondary Language: _____

6. Any Special Needs: _____

7. Social Media Usage: _____

8. Other: _____

Your Venue:

☐ In-school

☐ After-school

☐ Summer camp

☐ Church

☐ Home School

☐ Corporate

☐ Non Profit

☐ Government

Your Timeframe:

☐ Immediately   ☐ Next School Year

☐ Next Six Months   ☐ Uncertain (Exploring Possibilities)

Your WagiLabs Sessions:

of sessions, you would like: _____   Length of sessions: _____

Tell Us about Your Organization, School, or Club:

1. Your mission:

2. Your teachers, coaches, parents who will facilitate WagiLabs:

3. Would you like virtual WagiLabs training for your facilitators?

   ☐ Yes   ☐ No

4. Do you have reliable internet access?

   ☐ Yes   ☐ Skype

   ☐ No   ☐ FaceTime

5. Do you have resources to print graphic posters and supply prototype building supplies?

   ☐ Yes   ☐ No

6. Will you be able to find two to three coaches to help with the GuppyTank pitch?

   ☐ Yes   ☐ No

7. Are you interested in entering your kids' ideas in the "Ideas for Good" Contest? It's a global competition with a chance of winning $250 per selected idea and getting amazing social media coverage for your kids and their ideas?

   ☐ Yes   ☐ No

8. Can you send us signed Parent Consent Forms for the kids?

   ☐ Yes   ☐ No

Thank you very much!

Please email this Intake Form to woof@wagilabs.org

Pre-Launch Guide

Launch Questions:

1. What are the learning goals you hope to accomplish?

2. Why do you want to achieve these outcomes?

3. How can you help your kids uncover community challenges?

4. How many hours do you have to accomplish your learning?

5. What days and times work best for holding your sessions?

6. What sections of the playbook will you prioritize?

7. What time/place would be best for kids to pitch their ideas?

Prioritizing Playbook Activities:

Program Length	Activity	Sharing Kids' Ideas
5-10 hours	Being a Detective Walking in Others' Shoes Uncovering Needs Brainstorming Ideas	Post on social media Share with community Share with other kids
11-20 hours	Being a Detective Walking in Others' Shoes Uncovering Needs Brainstorming Ideas Prototyping Pitching Practice	Post on social media Share with community Share with other kids Pen pal opportunities
24+ hours	All 13 Sessions plus Pitching at GuppyTank Implementing Solutions Playing it Forward	Post on social media Share with community Share with other kids Pitch ideas Collaborate with other teams Global pen pal opportunities Ideas for Humanity Challenge

Using the Playbook:

1. You can print and make copies of desired pages, depending on which sections you choose to facilitate.

2. Use the **WagiCheer** at the beginning or end of each of your sessions. The cheer builds excitement and ownership of the WagiKids experience.

3. The **WagiVoyage** poster can be printed, displayed and reviewed during each of your sessions to keep the kids focused, on track, and motivated to reach their end goal.

4. The **WagiLabs Certificate** can be printed and distributed to each child in your group to celebrate their commitment to creating ideas that make the world a better place!

Sharing Your Kids' Ideas:

1. A great way to have fun connecting with other kids is to print or draw your own "**FlatWagi**." You can take pictures of your FlatWagi in different places in your community, or you could mail it to other WagiLabs groups, along with a description of your ideas and request feedback.

2. You can set up a **GuppyTank** opportunity for your kids to pitch their ideas to a panel of judges that will provide feedback. You could offer a monetary prize, invite local press, provide mentorship, and guidance for making their project real.

3. Share kids' ideas on social media by tagging @wagilabs.

4. We are looking to fund kids' ideas with our **"Ideas for Good"** Contest. To participate, your kids will need to complete the Prototype, Pitch, and GuppyTank sections of the playbook. Have the kids create a short video pitch about their idea and upload it to us.

Our WagiTeam

Chic Thompson

Chic is a fellow at the University of Virginia's Darden Business School and adjunct faculty at the Brookings Institution. In 2001, Harvard Business School released a case study on the speaking career of Chic entitled "What a Great Idea!." Chic's first book, "What a Great Idea!," published by HarperCollins, was a main selection  of the Executive Book Club. His second book, "Yes, But..." is a guide to overcoming the bureaucratic language that stifles continuous innovation. Chic worked in new product development and marketing for W.L. Gore and Associates (Gore-Tex®), Johnson & Johnson and Walt Disney.

Sandy Damashek

A pioneer in children's interactive media, Sandy helped launch the Interactive Group at Sesame Workshop. Since then, she has been at the forefront of digital media, producing and writing the  preschool channel of AT&T's interactive TV trial, producing interactive movies for The Amazing Space children's museum, collaborating on the Word World app for Play TV's mobile platform, and serving as Creative Producer for math-based Umigo appisodes. She has written more than 30 non fiction and fiction children's books.

James Orrigo

James works with kids battling cancer and is bridging the gap between the hospital room and the classroom through music, animation and video storytelling. www.ladinabattle.com

Lexi Hutchins

Lexi is a visual storyteller, passionate about helping organizations know their purpose and carry it out. www.tomboycreative.com

Julia Lin

Julia spent a year in rural Ghana volunteering at the community nonprofit Cocoa360. She started the Tarkwa Breman Girls' School WagiLabs program, where the second graders became health champions in their community through songwriting (https://tinyurl.com/everydaywash) and peer education. She is passionate about the role of design in improving lives.

Jennifer McKendree

Jen is the associate vice president of student programs at Operation Smile, a nonprofit that provides free surgeries around the world to children born with cleft palates. She has 16 years of public school experience as a middle school gifted science teacher and a school administrator, leading the International Baccalaureate Middle Years Program in Virginia Beach, Virginia.

Emmanuel Abebrese

Emmanuel was born in Ghana where he spent most of his teen years accompanying his parents on mission trips to rural communities. He developed a passion to serve the less privileged and has sought effective ways of helping those in need. Emmanuel established Citadel Foundation for Kids (CFK) as a non profit organization in Ghana and in the United States to collaborate their resources toward a better world for children.

Mary Porter Green

Mary is founder and president of Curiosity Zone Science and co-founder of Ever Wonder Records. Mary wonders about everything and puts her child-like sensibility into all that she does. When Mary started building Curiosity Zone in 2002, she was determined to be surrounded by children, geeking out about science, and making the world a better place.

Made in the USA
Monee, IL
31 October 2020